MW01593323

Integrated Disability Management

AN EMPLOYER'S GUIDE

Integrated Disability Management

AN EMPLOYER'S GUIDE

Janet R. Douglas

International Foundation
of Employee Benefit Plans

The opinions expressed in this book are those of the authors. The International Foundation of Employee Benefit Plans disclaims responsibility for views expressed and statements made in books published by the Foundation.

Edited by Mary Jo Brzezinski, CEBS

Copies of this book may be obtained from:
Publications Department
International Foundation of Employee Benefit Plans
18700 West Bluemound Road
P.O. Box 69
Brookfield, Wisconsin 53008-0069
(262) 786-6710, ext. 8240

Payment must accompany order.
Call (888) 33-IFEBP, option 4, for price information.

Published in 2000 by the International Foundation of Employee Benefit Plans, Inc.
©2000 International Foundation of Employee Benefit Plans, Inc.
All rights reserved.
Library of Congress Catalog Card Number: 99-64589
ISBN 0-89154-534-4
Printed in the United States of America

1M-799

Table of Contents

Acknowledgments

I would like to express my sincere thanks to everyone who contributed to this book. I would especially like to recognize my colleagues at IntegraComp, Sedgwick CMS, Marsh Risk Consulting, Partners In Performance, Nucleus, LLC and Gardner, Carton & Douglas for sharing their knowledge and insights so generously and for offering both helpful suggestions and constructive criticism.

There is one special person, without whom the book never would have materialized—Nancy Qutub. Thank you, Nancy, for your tireless editing, writing and rewriting, and for making *Integrated Disability Management—An Employer's Guide* a reality.

About the Authors

Janet R. Douglas is the Employment Risk Services Practice Leader for Marsh Risk Consulting. She was formerly president of IntegraComp, a division of Sedgwick Claims Management Services. Ms. Douglas specializes in the design and evaluation of programs to manage occupational and nonoccupational disability. Her most recent activities include developing and implementing cost containment, disability management and return-to-work programs for large insurance companies, TPAs and employers. Additionally, Ms. Douglas consults in the integration of workers' compensation, LTD and STD programs. She also designs injury prevention, wellness and health education programs. Ms. Douglas consults to employers, insurance companies, physicians and attorneys in the management of occupational injuries and illnesses. A frequent presenter at national conventions, Ms. Douglas has authored numerous articles and a textbook on managed workers' compensation. She received a master's of public health from the University of Illinois at the Medical Center, and a dual diploma in occupational therapy for physical dysfunction and psychiatry from St. Andrew's College of Occupational Therapy, England. Ms. Douglas is also a charter member of the American Society of Hand Therapists and a board member of the Integrated Benefits Institute.

Nancy C. Qutub is a communication specialist for Marsh Risk Consulting. Concentrating on the quality of written business products, she edits proposals, reports, technical papers, articles and marketing brochures. Ms. Qutub, who was previously employed at IntegraComp, has used her teaching experience for IDM projects that involve focus groups, interviews and surveys. Ms. Qutub graduated Phi Beta Kappa from Lake Forest College with a B.A. in English. She has completed 30 graduate-level credits in English and education at the University of Wisconsin.

Bruce L. Douglas is a senior consultant for Employment Risk Services at Marsh Risk Consulting. Dr. Douglas specializes in preventive medicine in the workplace with concentration in the health of older workers. Experienced in developing and supervising injury management and health care programs for large industrial facilities, he has conducted a program in occupational health for the City of Chicago and directed a division of the Illinois Department of Public Health. He has also developed and supervised multispecialty facilities for the treatment of chronic pain. Dr. Douglas served for four years in the Illinois General Assembly and two years as a Fulbright Professor in Japan. Dr. Douglas earned a doctorate of dental surgery from New York University, a master's of public health from the University of California and a master's in education from Columbia University. He graduated with an A.B. from Princeton University and is a diplomate of The American Board of Oral and Maxillofacial Surgery

Keith M. Higdon, a senior consultant at Employment Risk Services and formerly the research manager for IntegraComp LLC, specializes in program evaluation and survey research methods. His work in program evaluation focuses on impact assessments for claims management processes and initiatives in workers' compensation, integrated disability management (IDM) and absence management. Survey projects focus on both client and employee satisfaction and industry trends. He has trained hundreds of interviewers for survey data collection and presented numerous lectures in academic settings. Mr. Higdon's most recent work includes the evaluation of managed care initiatives, a national survey of risk managers and human resource directors regarding IDM, and the development of IDM and absence management programs. Mr. Higdon graduated with a B.S. in sociology and a B.S. in anthropology from Northern Illinois University in 1994. He received the ISO 9000 Lead Assessor Training Certificate in 1997 and is currently an M.A. candidate in sociology at Northern Illinois University.

John S. O'Connor II is a vice president at Reliance National where he is responsible for marketing integrated disability and medical products as well as assisting clients with implementation of their integrated programs. Prior to joining Reliance National, Dr. O'Connor was a senior vice president at Sedgwick Claims Management Services and responsible for the development and marketing of Sedgwick CMS's integrated services. In addition to his expertise in integrated programs, Dr. O'Connor–an exercise physiologist by education–has over 20 years experience in human factors research and performance training. For the past several years, he has been involved in researching the human factors that affect job performance, injury and return to work, as well as the role of corporate leadership during times of change. Dr. O'Connor earned his Ph.D. in exercise physiology from Arizona State University in 1987. He received a master's degree in education in 1980 from the University of Kansas, where he also completed his undergraduate work in social studies in 1970. He is a fellow of the American College of Sports Medicine.

Kathleen A. Rickert is a senior vice president at Employment Risk Services of Marsh Risk Consulting. She was a principal and founder of IntegraComp LLC. Ms. Rickert's experience includes consulting on workers' compensation injury-management and cost containment programs, workplace health, return-to-work programs and related regulatory issues (such as the Americans with Disabilities Act and the Family and Medical Leave Act). She has assisted clients with development and implementation of ergonomics programs, including worksite analyses and training. Most recently, Ms. Rickert developed an integrated disability management (IDM) assessment tool used to help clients ascertain their readiness for an IDM program. Ms. Rickert graduated magna cum laude from Mount Mary College with a B.S. in occupational therapy. She has earned her associate in risk management.

Timothy J. Stanton is an associate in the Employee Benefits Department of the Chicago office of Gardner, Carton & Douglas. His practice covers general employee benefits issues and has focused on health insurance, flexible benefit and other welfare benefit programs, including funding, design and legal compliance issues. He has spoken and written on issues including long-term care insurance and welfare benefit legislation and regulation. Mr. Stanton is a 1994 graduate of the Loyola University School of Law, where he was an editor at large of the *Loyola University Chicago Law Journal*. He received a bachelor of arts degree in journalism and political science with honors from the University of Wisconsin in 1988.

John W. Stimson has been working in the field of disability management since 1990. He has managed short- and long-term disability claims and worked as a vocational rehabilitation counselor. In 1991, Mr. Stimson created the Assessment, Coaching and Training Center (dedicated to the development of job transition skills for disabled workers) of Southern California Edison Company. He assumed management of the Disability Services Department in 1994 and headed a team to develop an integrated disability management program. In 1997, Mr. Stimson joined Sedgwick of Illinois as vice president and project manager of the Ameritech Disability Service Center, a dedicated integrated disability management program. Mr. Stimson is currently a senior vice president with Sedgwick and the regional operations director for the West Region, based in San Francisco. Mr. Stimson received his bachelor of arts degree from Western Michigan University in 1968. He is certified as a disability analyst by the American Board of Disability Analysts.

David L. Wolfe is a partner in the Chicago office of the law firm of Gardner, Carton & Douglas. He chairs its Employee Benefits Department and engages in a broad-based practice covering tax-qualified plans, health and welfare arrangement, and executive compensation. His subspecialties include benefits issues in corporate acquisitions and divestitures, benefits issues for tax-exempt clients, U.S. benefits for international clients, ERISA litigation, cash balance and other hybrid pensions arrangements, legal compliance review and nonqualified deferred compensation arrangements. Mr. Wolfe received his J.D., cum laude, from the University of Michigan in 1976. He is a 1973 graduate of the University of Illinois, and has been a certified public accountant since 1973.

Preface

by David A. North
President
Sedgwick Claims
Management Services

Throughout history, employers have striven to influence the productivity of employees. They've tried physical persuasion, mental corruption, mental collusion and moral obligation. What all these approaches have in common is an attempt to bridge employee needs with employer wants. In recent times, employers have figured out that employees need a sense of belonging, personal recognition and financial compensation; but seeing fulfillment of these needs merely as a necessary burden to doing business tends to work only minimally, while undermining morale.

The alternative to such a negative approach is to recognize the needs and wants as only objectives, and to structure an environment that encourages behavior that supports the goals. The early results of integrated disability management (IDM) programs show that goals are being addressed in a positive manner. Employers are motivated to provide a safe and healthy workplace and create an environment where the employee's total worth is reinforced by the employer's desire to return injured employees to work.

The concept of integrating the employer's voluntary and statutory benefits plans into an efficient system to meet the employee's needs and the company's wants is only the beginning of the bridge. Now, just when IDM concepts are taking hold, the focus has broadened to *absence management*–recognizing that the fundamental processes behind IDM's effectiveness are equally beneficial to casual absences like sick time and the Family and Medical Leave Act (FMLA). Early, effective medical interventions, complemented with tailored modified-duty programs and coordination of procedures and benefits, extend the bridge between employee needs and employer wants. This expansion of the now-traditional IDM concept will gain greater momentum as FMLA enforcement increases and employers begin to bear its full legal and administrative complexity.

The land beyond absence management may be even greener. The total health productivity management approach, in addition to bringing group health issues into the disability equation, positions the corporate administrators of these programs to aid the business mission, not just minimize the loss. The fundamentals of preloss injury prevention, the health of workers, and postinjury/illness medical treatment apply to all employee injuries and illness, work related and nonwork related alike. Improving the effectiveness of medical care is equally beneficial in workers' compensation and group health.

Merging the workers' compensation, disability, group health and administrative leaves could be just the groundwork for the real changes we will see. The traditional separation of risk management and employee benefits, which has served us well in the development stage, must give way to strategies that promote growth, not just prevent loss. Corporations that see the value of productivity over disability will complete the bridge between employee needs and employer wants. For these companies, fulfilling employee needs will cease to be a necessary burden and become an indispensable use of available resources to generate profit.

Once the trend has been set, the restructuring of the industry will continue in earnest. The marketplace will respond with the reinvention of supplier companies no longer identified with only property/casualty or only life and health. Regulators will see the wisdom of removing licensing requirements and statutory barriers that force innovators to appear compliant (through fronts and marketing trickery) in order to act progressively. The educational community will respond with programs that teach the fundamentals of medical management, disability management, productivity enhancement and integrated thinking, rather than coverage certification.

Industry leaders are already changing the landscape–one hill at a time–with innovative new strategies. To aid the next generation of practitioners in routing their integration strategies, Janet R. Douglas, an experienced consultant in workers' compensation, disability and absence management, and her co-authors have begun to develop a road map. With the approach described in *Integrated Disability Management–An Employer's Guide,* corporations can see the financial and human capital benefits of a workforce that is *productivity* focused, and progress toward the optimal state of total health and productivity management.

Foreword

by Janet R. Douglas

Integrated disability management (IDM) is one of the topics most widely discussed among human resource and risk management consultants, health care and administrative service providers, and employers. Everyone seems to agree that it makes sense to treat occupational and nonoccupational illness and injury the same way and to have consistent policies to expedite return to work and payment for lost time regardless of cause. However, few employers find themselves in a situation where they can readily embrace the new concepts of disability management and move forward quickly, because of the tangled web of contracts, policies, procedures, turf, past practices and multiple service providers that surrounds their health, workers' compensation and disability programs.

Employers, typically, have not arrived at their current state as a result of a plan or strategy but rather as a result of reaction to a series of events–social, political and contractual–over most of this century. Forces external and internal to the company have required employer responsibility for employee health care, compensation for work-related injury and illness, accommodation of individuals with disabilities and, now, authorized leave to take care of family issues and personal health problems.

Employers find themselves in a situation where they confront increasingly complex statutory requirements, extraordinarily complicated and convoluted health and disability plans, ever-increasing costs, too few people to do the work and a workforce that is aging rapidly. No wonder a simple, strategic approach to managing health and lost time looks attractive. Clearly IDM offers a major step in the right direction, but how to get there remains the challenge.

The purpose of this book is to offer practical help to the employer in understanding its current state and in developing a vision and an action plan for moving forward: first to IDM and, ultimately, to total health management. To help the employer understand the context for integration, Chapter One presents historical background and Chapter Two defines IDM; Chapters Three (drivers of disability costs) and Four (legal liabilities) address the more universal issues that guide an employer not only while investigating program options but also while implementing and evaluating them. Chapters Five through Eight describe the actions employers should take to assess their current state and to implement and evaluate process changes.

Section I

Introduction

I n the early 1990s, the pros and cons of the Clinton administration's "24-hour" health care reform plan were being hotly debated. Proponents pointed out the value of occupational and non-occupational medical care *integration*–quality care for all, regardless of the cause of injury. Opponents countered that medical care integration would result in a *disintegrated* approach to occupational disability management. They argued that carriers would favor less costly conservative intervention and deny coverage for treatments that, while more expensive, could speed an employee's recovery and return to work. Though this approach might contain medical costs, it would certainly increase disability costs (i.e., indemnity payments for lost time and indirect costs for training, replacement workers, decreased productivity, etc.)

Chapter 1

A Historical Perspective on Integration

by Kathleen A. Rickert

As debate continued, private industry recognized the possibility that reform could be mandated. Consultants, employers and insurers began to explore how integration might work. Though support for Clinton's plan dwindled and finally disappeared, industry reached a different conclusion: Not only could integration work, it made sense (although, at least initially, in a different form than the Clinton plan).

Major consulting firms advised their clients to pursue integration in order to simplify their benefit programs, improve quality and reduce cost. Employers, ever open to ways of increasing their profit margins, started to evaluate their readiness for integration as a means of reducing overhead. Recognizing that integration would also allow them to provide better benefits, employers realized this would, in turn, allow them to compete more effectively for a dwindling workforce. In order to meet customers' demands for integration solutions, workers' compensation and disability insurers and claims administrators began to develop alliances with each other and, in some cases, one-vendor integration products.

Although debate regarding Clinton's proposed health care reform plan was the immediate impetus for these initiatives, periodic debate over national health care has been waged since the early part of this century. It is important to have a basic understanding of this history–the waxing and waning of support for health care reform as well as the piecemeal evolution of state workers' compensation and federal health care and disability programs–to fully appreciate the challenges and opportunities presented by today's integration efforts.

A national health insurance movement was afoot as early as the second decade of the 1900s. Although employers were initially supportive, they began to fear unforeseen costs after it became evident that recently introduced workers' compensation programs would be more expensive than originally expected. Business support subsided, labor support was at best lukewarm, and organized medicine and private insurance were actively opposed. The final nail–World War I–left the public openly antagonistic toward anything they perceived as "Germanic," and Germany had introduced national health insurance in the late 1800s.

In the 1930s, I.S. Falk, the research counsel for the Social Security Board, criticized both the distinction made between occupational and nonoccupational disability and the quality of care available to injured workers. But reform was again thwarted by various interests (including private insurance and state administrators) that were opposed to a national health care program in favor of retaining state control of occupational disability programs. "Social welfare" amendments to the Social Security Act widened the gap between federal- and state-based health and disability programs. Federally funded vocational rehabilitation programs, which focused on returning the injured worker to gainful employment, failed to coalesce with state-controlled workers' compensation programs, which focused primarily on payment of lost wages.

In the 1940s, with the support of labor, liberal politicians and progressive farmers, President Harry S. Truman again called for a national health care plan. Once more, various interests opposed these efforts and, similar to the earlier anti-German sentiment, fear of the then-common enemy, Communism, prevented widespread support for "socialized medicine."

The call for reform resumed in the 1960s, at which time coverage for the elderly (through Medicare) and the poor (through Medicaid) was finally accomplished. The '70s and '80s saw significant changes in these programs as well as state workers' compensation programs. While the federal programs became more restrictive with the advent of diagnosis related groups, or DRGs (a prospective payment system), the state programs provided increasing medical coverage and experienced rising indemnity payments. Health care providers reacted by shifting costs from the less profitable federal payment programs as well as from the new capitated health maintenance organizations (HMOs) to the more liberal workers' compensation system. In response, self-insured employers and workers' compensation carriers began to adopt cost-containment strategies.[1]

As health care costs continued to rise, especially within the workers' compensation system,[2] there were increasing cries for reform in the form of integration of the current programs or an entirely new single delivery system. By 1990, the search for a better approach resulted in a 24-hour employee health care coverage option to satisfy workers' compensation requirements in Florida, and the study of, or recommendations for, the same in California, Minnesota, Alaska and Oregon.[3] By 1996, Colorado, Iowa, Kentucky, Louisiana, Maine, Massachusetts, Montana, North Carolina, Oklahoma and Washington also had developed regulations or laws setting the stage for 24-hour programs.[4]

This was the environment when Clinton's plan was proposed and rejected, and the industry decided to pursue integration without a government mandate. With the rising incidence of mental stress and cumulative trauma disorders that could be caused or at least aggravated by both work and nonwork activities, there was no longer a clear line separating occupational and nonoccupational injuries and illnesses. To complicate matters, the workers' compensation system had implemented cost-containment strategies, while nonoccupational disability programs went essentially unmanaged, encouraging cost shifting among the systems. DRGs, HMOs, PPOs and the rest of the alphabet soup of health care payment systems limited access to care for some; while others continued to pay higher insurance premiums for more extensive coverage and for the freedom to choose their own providers; and still others went without any coverage at all.

The solution industry formulated and larger employers began to demand was *integrated disability management* (IDM). With the goal of managing time lost from work (disability) consistently, regardless of whether an injury or illness was work related, IDM would tackle the problems of cost shifting, introduce cost-containment strategies to the nonoccupational disability system and begin to address inconsistencies in quality of care.

Without a template to follow, insurance carriers, third-party administrators and medical management companies have struggled to develop integrated solutions. Initially, large employers and their consultants went to market with requests for highly customized, employer-driven programs. Initial designs were sometimes overambitious or flawed and almost always failed to take into account the complex business environment in which changes were to be implemented. But, despite all the difficulties surrounding the initial efforts at integration, there was a sense that the effort would be worthwhile: Ultimately there would be improvement in quality, efficiency and employee satisfaction, and costs associated with both occupational and nonoccupational illness and injury would decline.

Today IDM is a fact of life, in varying forms and varying stages of implementation at many companies. Though IDM is still perceived as challenging and threatening in many organizations, its sheer commonsense appeal makes it a difficult concept to resist. The opportunity now exists for employers to take advantage of lessons learned by the pioneers in the field and to adopt a model of integration that allows them to improve quality and reduce cost.

Endnotes

1. Judith Greenwood, "A Historical Perspective on Workers' Compensation in the Context of the National Health Policy Debate," *Health Care Cost Containment*, edited by J. Greenwood and A. Tarricco (Horsham, PA: LRP Publications, 1992), 1-25.

2. John R. Burton, "National Health Care Reform and Workers' Compensation," *John Burton's Workers' Compensation Monitor*, November/December 1993, 3.

3. Alliance of American Insurers, 1-3.

4. R. Hergenrader and K. King, "Opportunities Expanding in 24-Hour Care Programs," *Best's Review*, May 1996, 66.

Like all new and emerging programs, IDM means different things to different people. There are, in fact, several definitions of *integration*. The definition most commonly used refers to integration of occupational and nonoccupational disability management, otherwise known as *workers' compensation, short-term disability (STD)* and *long-term disability (LTD)*.

Many employers began, however, by first integrating short- and long-term disability administration and then added workers' compensation at a later date. The intent was to remove those programs from the "silos" in which they had resided historically. (See Exhibit 2A.)

Each of the diagrams in Exhibit 2A shows a distinct variation of *horizontal integration*–that is, the integration of historically separate claims management systems or benefits. Two variations, absence management (Exhibit 2B) and total health management (Exhibit 2C), are actually hybrids, that is, mixtures of *horizontal* and *vertical integration* concepts.

Chapter 2
Definitions and Models for Integrated Disability Management (IDM)

by Kathleen A. Rickert and Janet R. Douglas

A system is *vertically integrated* when all programs related to illness and injury, from prevention through return to work, are coordinated. Vertical integration is based on the prevention continuum.

In a vertically integrated system, prevention responsibilities that have been historically fragmented among the medical department (wellness programs,

Exhibit 2A

HORIZONTAL INTEGRATION

Integration of Short-Term and Long-Term Disability

Integrated Disability Management

exposure testing), safety department (including job safety analyses, ergonomics and engineering) and human resources (hiring practices, pre-offer testing and job placement, etc.) are linked through communication and cross-training and redistribution of responsibilities.(See Appendix 2A.) Early intervention becomes the responsibility of the medical department or line supervisor on the scene as well as the employee, the claims administrator and the provider. (See Appendix 2B.) And rehabilitation efforts are managed by outside providers knowledgeable about the injured employee's job duties and claims adjusters who understand the medical issues and the availability of job accommodations. (See Appendix 2C.) Vertical integration, with its coordinated efforts and improved communication among the various groups, results in opportunities for injury prevention, disability reduction and cost control.

This book deals primarily with horizontal integration but advocates a horizontally integrated program within a vertically integrated system for maximum benefit to employer and employee.

Exhibit 2B

HORIZONTAL AND VERTICAL INTEGRATION— ABSENCE MANAGEMENT

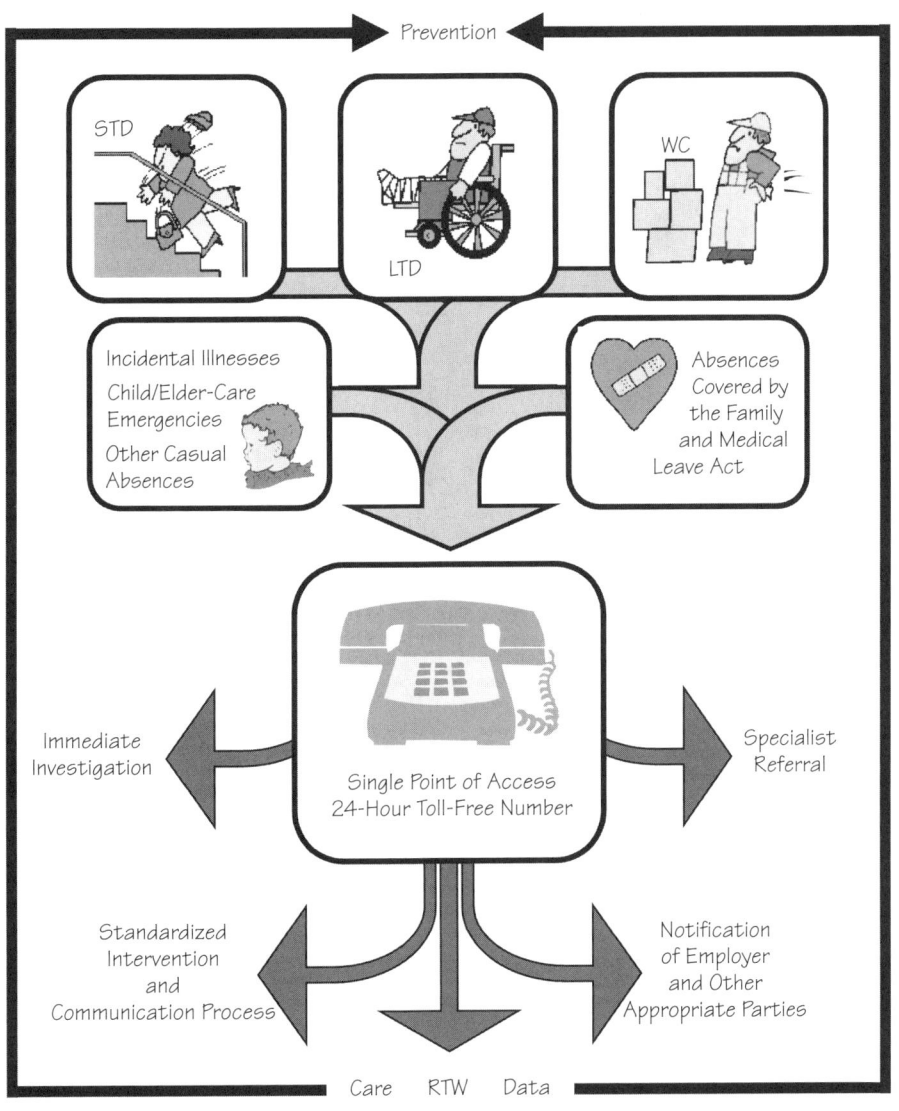

HORIZONTAL AND VERTICAL INTEGRATION—
TOTAL HEALTH MANAGEMENT

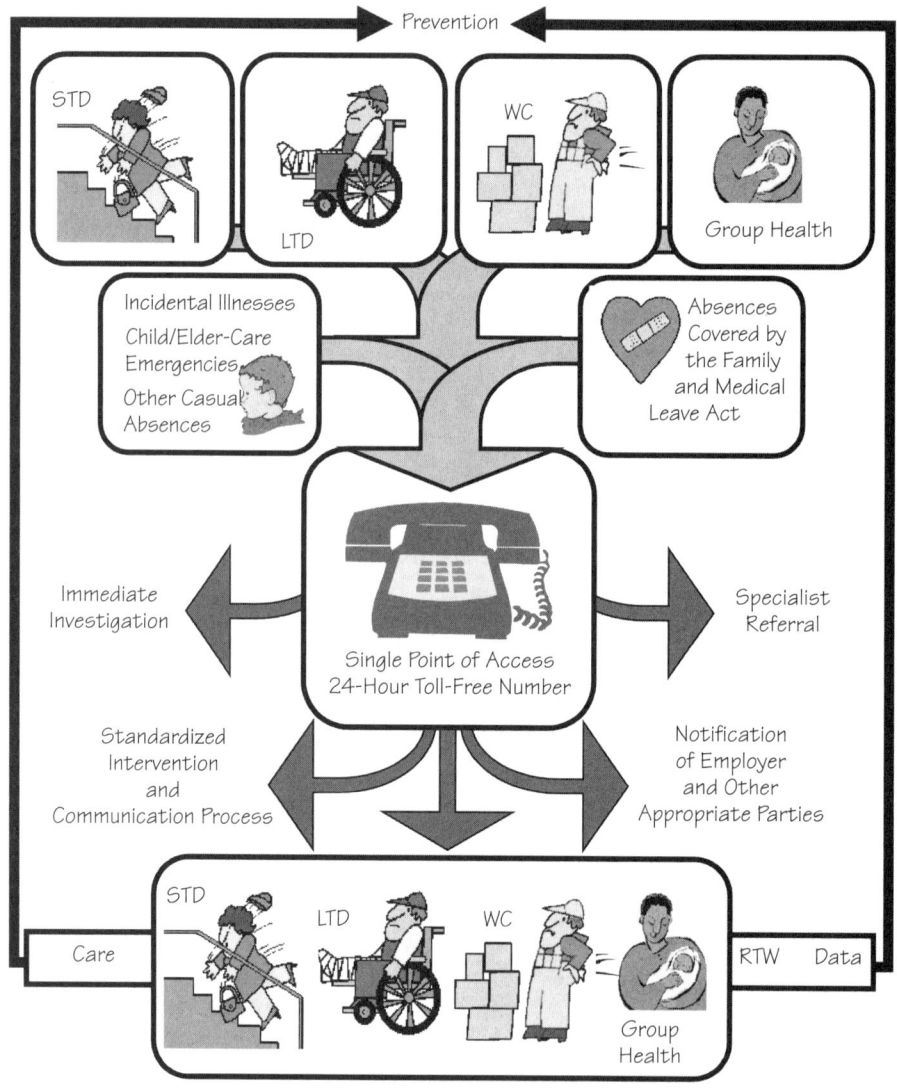

Integration of Short-
and Long-Term Disability

As previously mentioned, integration of nonoccupational disability programs is the earliest form integration takes for many employers and, therefore, the most common. This approach to integration has the following basic characteristics and goals:

◆ Streamlining of the management of nonoccupational disability, resulting in, among other things, increased customer (injured or ill employee) satisfaction

◆ Reduction in administrative costs, resulting in overall program savings

◆ Initiation of claims and care management at the earliest possible point, resulting in earlier return to work.

These goals are accomplished through a system that supports early notification of all interested parties; referral to appropriate care providers and case managers; ongoing monitoring or, if called for, active management and follow-up; benchmarking against disability duration guidelines and treatment protocols; and proactive return-to-work efforts.

Some employers are applying these same management techniques to nonoccupational injuries and illnesses that are of longer duration but fall short of STD. These absences are costly, in and of themselves, since the employer is paying for nonproductive time through sick days, salary continuation or paid-time-off plans. Cost savings, then, come from increased productivity brought about by earlier return to work. Because case management is begun at an earlier point, there is a reduction in cases that would have converted to STD or, at the very least, in STD durations.[1]

Integration of Short-
and Long-Term Disability
With Workers' Compensation—IDM

The next step toward full integration is integration of nonoccupational disability (LTD and STD) and occupational (workers' compensation) programs. The basic characteristics and goals of this approach to integration are:

◆ Consistency in the management of disabilities, resulting in increased customer (injured or ill employee) satisfaction and decreased exposure to litigation[2]

◆ Reduction in administrative costs, resulting in overall program savings

◆ Reduction in disability durations, resulting in improved productivity and related cost savings.[3]

These goals are accomplished through an integrated system that may take a variety of forms, but includes at least the following four elements:

1. *Common intake of claims:* All claims–STD, LTD and workers' compensation–are called into one toll-free number. Intake may be limited to gathering basic information that is then forwarded to the appropriate claims specialist, or it may include more specialized services such as provider referral and gathering of specific job information. Common intake saves costs through streamlined administration and prevention of double-dipping (filing of two claims for the same injury).

2. *Integrated medical management:* The injured/ill employee is referred to the appropriate provider (including specialists when necessary) in a timely manner. Integrated managed care uses the same medical treatment protocols regardless of whether the injury/illness is occupational or nonoccupational in nature, and it promotes a "shared philosophy of claim management and return to work between the claim managers and care providers."[4]

3. *"Equal opportunity" stay-at-work and return-to-work programs:* Employees who have medical conditions or injuries (regardless of cause) are enabled, whenever appropriate, to remain at work. All employees with or without medical restrictions, who are returning to work after a period of disability, are given the same return-to-work opportunities. Return to work is the focus of claims and case management and, therefore, addressed early and throughout the case.

4. *Integrated data management and reporting:* This is achieved either by a single system that manages claims for short- and long-term disability and workers' compensation or by "warehousing" of data to permit the use of multiple management systems. The former method is preferred, but expensive, and the warehousing option gives the ability to provide the integrated analysis and reporting that is vital to performance measurement.

Absence Management

While IDM is evolving, it is becoming apparent there is a problem inherent in the system with respect to early identification of nonoccupational disabilities. In workers' compensation the occurrence of an injury is usually known immediately and there can be true early intervention to promote rapid recovery and mitigate loss. However, because the medical portion of nonoccupational disability is covered by group health insurance, the IDM program would not be notified until an individual had reached the eligibility threshold for disability, which could be several weeks—frequently as many as 26 weeks after the onset or occurrence. Consequently, opportunities for early intervention and expedited return to work are lost. An emerging solution to this problem is found in the concept of absence management, where an employee must notify the employer, typically through a toll-free number, of all absences for whatever cause.

Absence management is a hybrid version of horizontal and vertical integration concepts. It is essentially a system for monitoring and controlling the use of unscheduled time off and of unpaid leaves related to the Family and Medical Leave Act. It is similar to other horizontally integrated programs because it deals with absences covered by different benefit programs. Absence management, however, is more inclusive in that it covers all nonvacation absences, whether related to an employee's incidental illness, STD, LTD or workers' compensation, or any other circumstance that keeps the employee from work, such as the illness of an employee's family member or the need for last-minute child care.

Absence management is similar to other vertically integrated programs because pre-loss through post-loss activities are coordinated. Absence management supports secondary and tertiary prevention by identifying and managing the root cause of an absence, and it supports primary prevention by collecting absence data and using it to identify wellness and other intervention programs that would prevent future absences.

The basic characteristics and goals of this approach to integration are:
- Better communication, which preserves confidentiality related to all employee absences and results in increased customer (injured or ill employee) satisfaction
- Reduction in administrative costs, which produces overall program savings
- Earlier referral for appropriate medical care and other resources, which reduces time-off incidences and disability durations and, consequently, improves productivity.

The following components are common to most absence management programs:
- Single point of access: Employees report absences or anticipated absences via a 24-hour toll-free number.
- Immediate investigation: The reason for absence is investigated, generally through a simple inquiry by intake personnel.
- Standardized intervention and communication process: The rea-

son for absence is determined and coded for tracking, and appropriate intervention is initiated using problem-related protocols and employer-specific benefits criteria. The intake person (or specialist, if appropriate) communicates the client-specific benefits information to the employee.

◆ Notification: The employer and all other appropriate parties are immediately notified of the absence. This may include the claims administrator and the state (e.g., First Report of Injury in workers' compensation cases), in addition to various individuals at the worksite, such as the immediate supervisor for purposes of scheduling, payroll for purposes of appropriate pay coding and occupational health nurse for purposes of facilitating return to work through functional job analysis.

◆ Specialist referral: Based on predetermined criteria, certain calls are referred to a specialist or clinician for further assessment, more in-depth discussion or referral to special resources.

Total Health Management

Total health management implies a comprehensive approach to the health needs of an employed population. Many employers have chosen to integrate other programs first, and often health care is the last benefit they plan to integrate. Nonetheless, research conducted with middle-sized employers shows they believe integration of group health is critical.[5] Meanwhile, service providers are beginning to offer plans that integrate STD, LTD, workers' compensation and group health,[6] with the addition of absence management concepts.

The basic characteristics and goals of this approach to integration are:

◆ Simplified administration of health benefits, regardless of cause of injury or illness, resulting in increased customer (injured or ill employee) satisfaction

◆ Reduction in costs related to shifting nonoccupational claims to the more profitable occupational side, resulting in savings

◆ Consistency in medical care and management of nonoccupational and occupational health claims, resulting in decreased disability durations (and a return-to-work focus for the nonoccupational claims) and, consequently, improved productivity

◆ Better communication, which preserves confidentiality related to all employee absences and results in increased customer (injured or ill employee) satisfaction.

Total health management should include the same basic elements as integrated disability programs, with variations because of the group health and absence management components:

- ◆ Common intake of claims: Workers' compensation and group health claims are called into the same number, and the employee or patient has the same contact regardless of type of claim.
- ◆ Integrated medical management: This includes contracting with medical providers for both group health and workers' compensation cases, and common care managers to coordinate care.
- ◆ Return-to-work focus: Since medical care is integrated, the approach to the injured or ill patient is more holistic, and work is a focus, whether the illness or injury is occupational or non-occupational.
- ◆ Single database: A single database allows for analysis of provider utilization, injury and illness trends and disability durations for all health-related issues.[7]

Models for Integrated Disability Management

While total health management has a great deal of merit, there is too little accumulated experience for this book to focus in that direction. IDM, beginning with short-term disability and culminating with the inclusion of group health, appears to be an evolutionary response to the employer's need to start the process somewhere. There are, in fact, several different routes for the employer to take.

The basic hypothesis of this book is there are four simple criteria that must be met in order for a program to be considered integrated.

1. Integrated intake: Employees report their illness, injury or casual absence to a single toll-free telephone number or e-mail address as specified by the employer.
2. Integrated care: Medical care is of consistent quality and cost, and follows the same treatment protocols, regardless of origin of illness or injury.
3. Equal opportunity to return to work: Disability durations are consistent, with absence determined by inability to meet the physical and psychological demands of available work.
4. Integrated reporting: Reports are comprehensive (encompassing the total disability picture) and readable. They provide meaningful, usable information to the employer that evaluates both the program and vendor performance.

Having determined that those four criteria can be met, the employer has several options with respect to program design and implementation. First, however, a series of questions need to be answered (based upon careful analysis of existing programs) about the financing of risks associated with workers' compensation and short- and long-term disability. Are the current programs insured, self-insured, self-administered or a combination of all of the above? Are there multiple service providers involved in managing existing programs? Are workers' compensation costs under control?

There is no one-size-fits-all model for IDM. Thorough analysis of a company's current state, history and culture will point to a model that best meets an employer's needs. There are, however, key decisions that drive model design, and they need to be made before the search for the ideal program begins. Will the IDM program be customized or off the shelf? Will it be centralized or decentralized? Will it be clinically or administratively driven? And, finally, will the IDM program be managed in-house or outsourced to an insurance company or third-party administrator? Issues to consider in making these decisions follow.

Customized or Off the Shelf

To date, most large employers (25,000+ employees) are opting for highly customized IDM programs. These programs are individualized, staff intensive and expensive in terms of initial outlay—though early results indicate they are cost effective. The employer has typically worked with a consultant to design specifications, issued a request for proposal and hired one or more service providers to manage the program. The customized program requires considerable time and energy on the part of the employer but, if designed appropriately, meshes well with company culture.

Smaller employers or those with less ability or interest in deploying in-house resources to the IDM initiative will, typically, opt for an "off-the-shelf" program. This should be a best-practice program that has been designed by a service provider, leaning on lessons learned from experience with customized programs. Off-the-shelf programs offer few options to the employer but take advantage of both volume and efficiency of process to offer comprehensive, cost effective service.

Centralized or Decentralized

Companies generally have management styles that can be described as either centralized or decentralized. Centralization can imply management from a single corporate location of multiple divisions or plants across a broad geographic area, or of multiple divisions or subsidiaries that may be involved in different businesses that may or may not be geographically dispersed. Decentralized management means divisions or subsidiary companies operating with strong local autonomy and minimal corporate involvement. IDM programs can be run along similar lines.

Most of the early IDM programs are centralized, with claims being managed at a single location. Where necessary, jurisdiction-specific input (such as workers' compensation benefit information) is obtained outside of the disability management center and fed to it either electronically or telephonically. Attempting to impose centralized disability management on a strongly decentralized culture is a barrier to implementation of IDM, and has given rise to more "decentralized" thinking among service providers. Customized programs, although usually centralized, can be offered on a decentralized basis. Off-the-shelf models are almost always centralized or regionalized.

Clinical or Administrative

IDM requires both meaningful clinical management and highly skilled claims administration. Employers have shown preferences for different approaches based on which skill set features more prominently in their programs. Some models feature a clinician, usually a registered nurse, as the first point of contact for employees who call to report an injury or illness. Nurses' training and experience allow them to perform early triage, recognize signs and symptoms of a potentially serious condition, answer employees' medically related questions and make appropriate referrals. Having been involved with employees from the onset, appropriately trained nurses can begin disability management earlier and shorten disability durations.

The administrative model puts a senior claims professional at the heart of the program. That individual is charged with the responsibility of determining whether or not a clinical case manager is required and what level of claims expertise is needed to achieve the best possible outcome.

There is no right or wrong approach. At their best, both models work well. Initially there was concern that the clinical model–resting heavily on nurses, who are a costly resource–would be more expensive. This is the case in some circumstances, but there is evidence that shows that early involvement of a nurse can dramatically improve the overall outcome. The key factors for the employer in making a choice appear once again to be compatibility with company philosophy and culture and availability of internal resources such as a well-staffed medical department. (See Exhibits 2D and 2E, Employer Options for IDM.)

Exhibit 2D

EMPLOYER OPTIONS FOR IDM (MODELS)

Customized or Off the Shelf
Key Decisions—Centralized or Decentralized
Clinical or Administrative

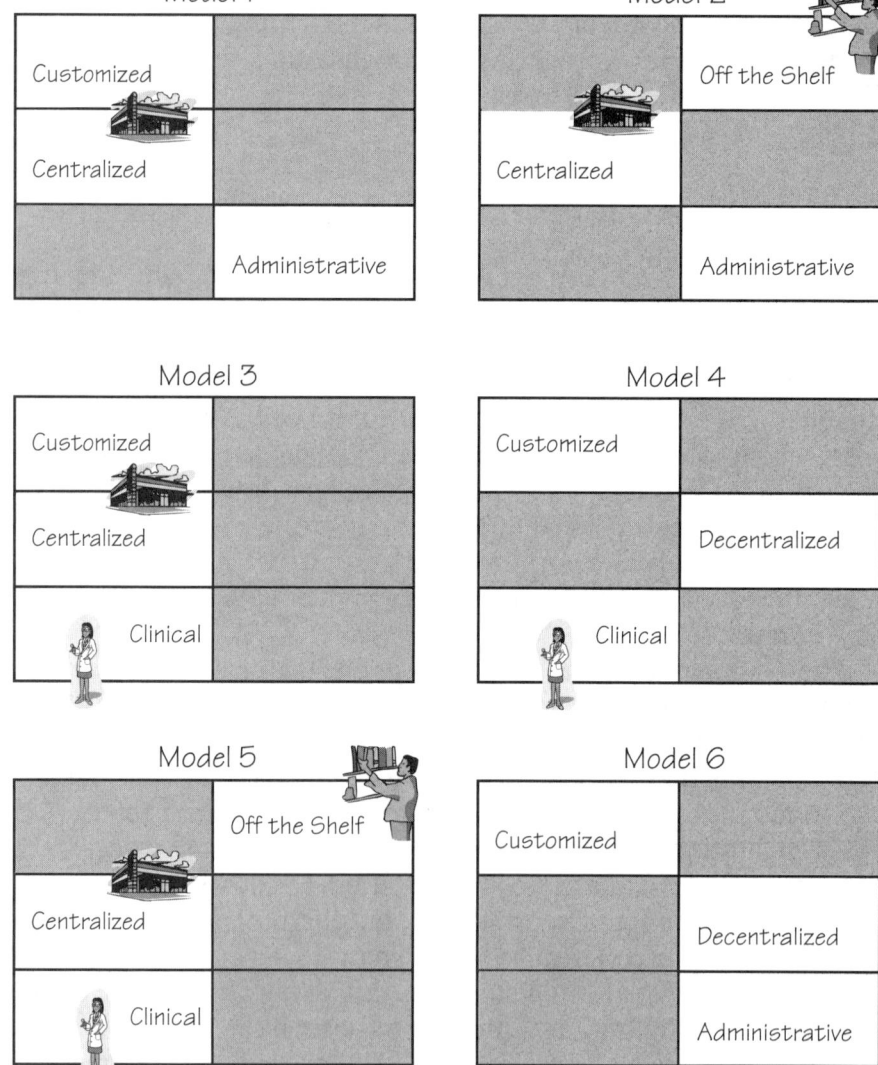

Exhibit 2E

EMPLOYER OPTIONS FOR IDM—
THE INTEGRATION CONTINUUM

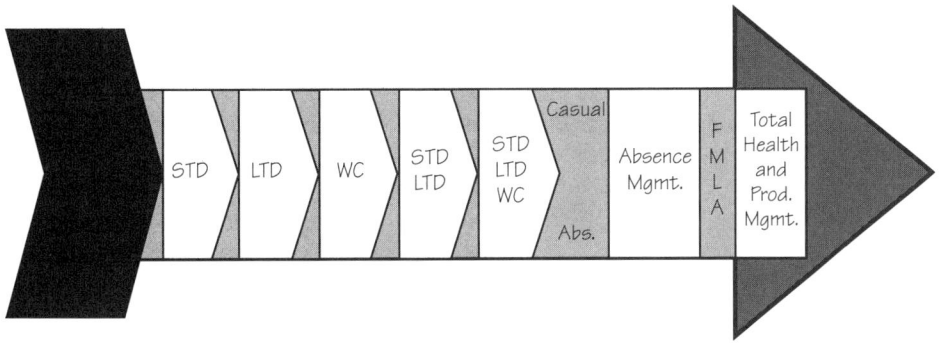

Other Critical Decisions

The employer must determine whether IDM will be handled in-house or outsourced. Most models call for outsourcing some part of the program, but the employer may retain control of certain functions.

Regardless of the model chosen and the degree to which it is handled in-house, it is vital to integrate fully the four basic functions–common intake, medical management, equal opportunity to return to work and information management. If the employer takes a systematic and thorough approach to determining readiness for IDM (see Chapter 5), the template for the most appropriate model will emerge.

The employer must also decide whether IDM should be insured or self-insured, in which the size of the company is clearly a factor. For the large employer that already self-insures workers' compensation and short- and/or long-term disability, the decision may be simple. For others it may be necessary to insure fully or to purchase a combination of insured and self-insured services. IDM has less to do with the underwriting of loss and much more to do with its efficient management; an employer can proceed without necessarily changing every aspect of existing insurance programs.

Endnotes

1. Randall K. Abbott, "The Business Case for Integrated Benefits," *Journal of Compensation and Benefits,* May/June 1997, 61.

2. Consistency in management minimizes exposure to litigation related to the Americans with Disabilities Act, and increased customer satisfaction decreases the possibility that an employee covered by workers' compensation will retain legal counsel.

3. D. North and K. Higdon, "Integration: Why You Need It, How to Get It," *The Journal of Workers' Compensation,* Fall 1996, 39-40.

4. Ibid., 41-43.

5. Ibid., 9.

6. Linda Koco, "24-Hour Plan Offers Health, Disability, and Workers' Comp.," *National Underwriter,* 2 March 1998, 29-30.

7. R. Hergenrader and K. King, "Opportunities Expanding in 24-Hour Care Programs," *Best's Review,* May 1996, 66-67.

Appendix 2A

VERTICAL INTEGRATION–PRIMARY PREVENTION

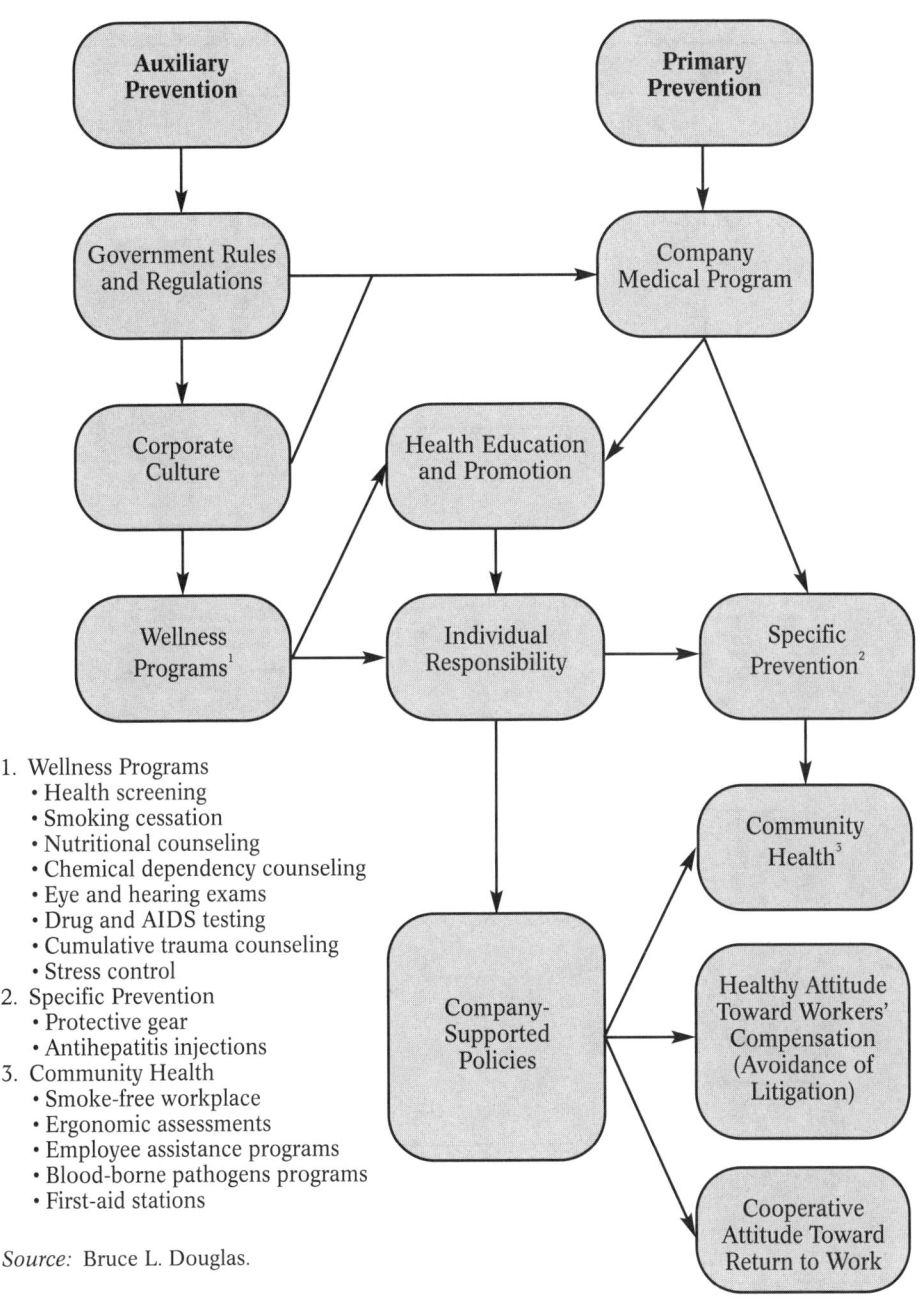

1. Wellness Programs
   • Health screening
   • Smoking cessation
   • Nutritional counseling
   • Chemical dependency counseling
   • Eye and hearing exams
   • Drug and AIDS testing
   • Cumulative trauma counseling
   • Stress control
2. Specific Prevention
   • Protective gear
   • Antihepatitis injections
3. Community Health
   • Smoke-free workplace
   • Ergonomic assessments
   • Employee assistance programs
   • Blood-borne pathogens programs
   • First-aid stations

Source: Bruce L. Douglas.

Appendix 2B

VERTICAL INTEGRATION–SECONDARY PREVENTION

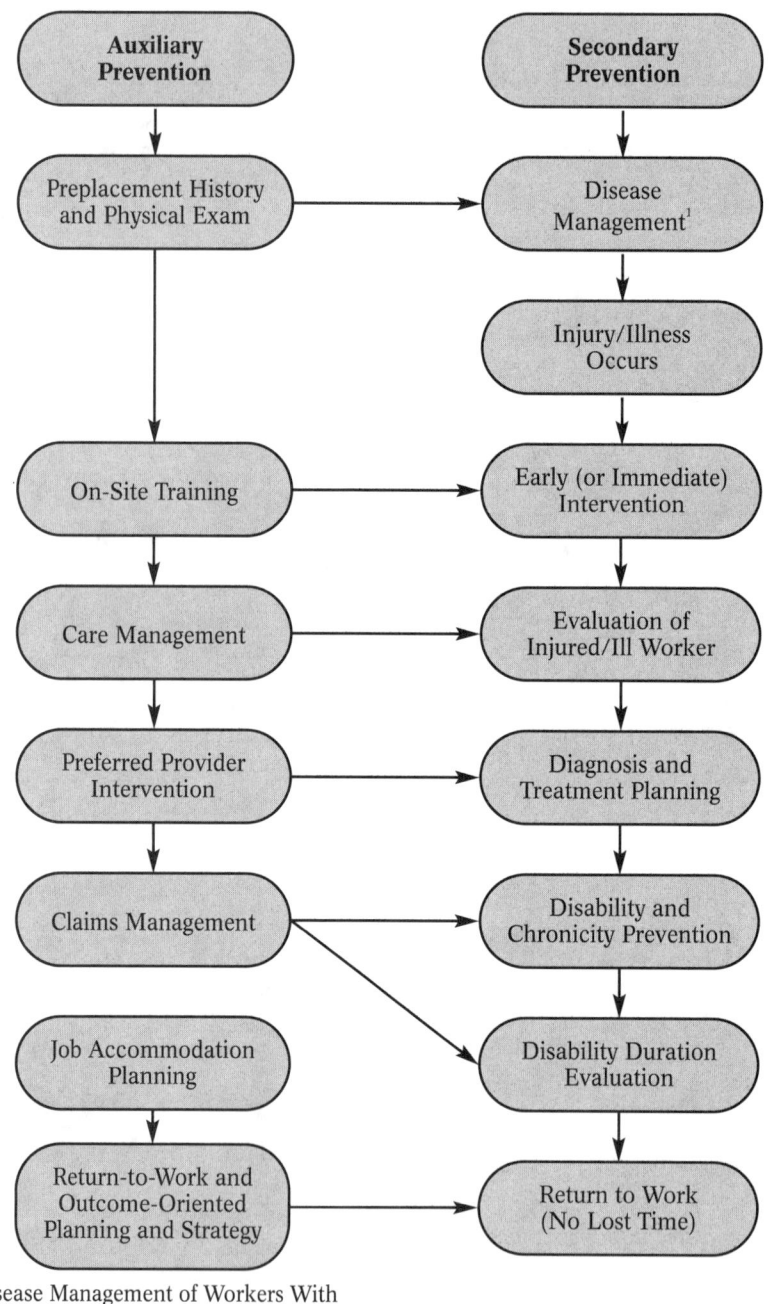

1. Disease Management of Workers With
   - Diabetes
   - Allergies
   - Musculoskeletal or other pain
   - Asthma
   - Hypertension
   - Medication management

Source: Bruce L. Douglas.

Appendix 2C

VERTICAL INTEGRATION–TERTIARY PREVENTION

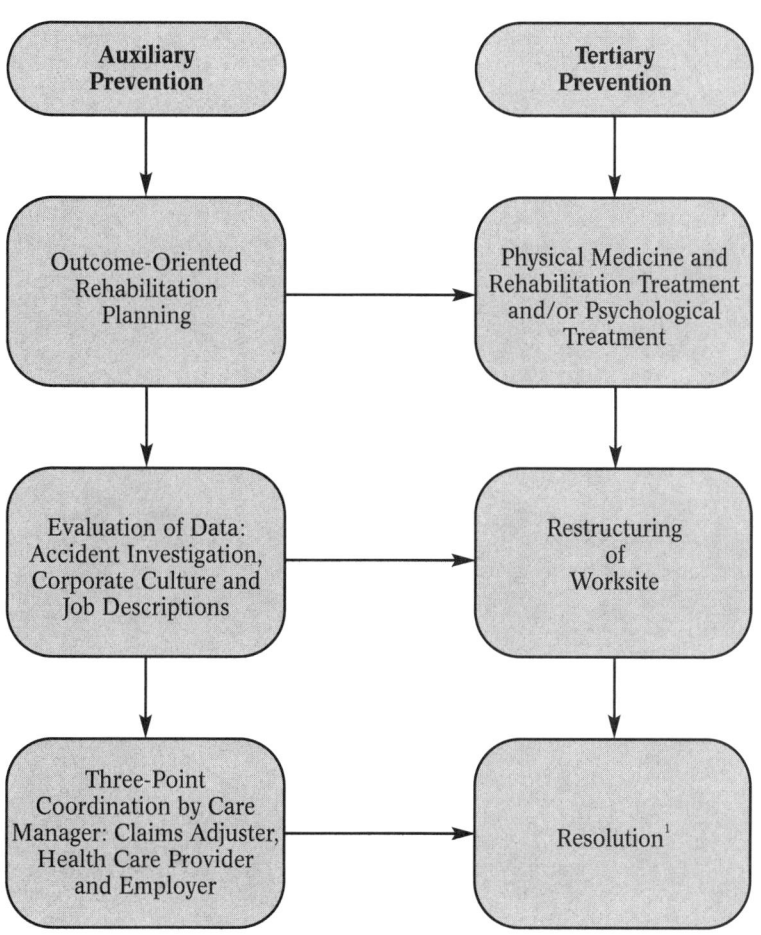

1. Resolutions include
   • Return to work
   • Disability management
   • Home-based services
   • Chronic pain programs
   • Community re-entry
Approximately 90% of all workers return to work within 90 days of injury/illness;
the remaining 10% are referred for disability management.

Source: Bruce L. Douglas.

Section II

Preliminary Concerns

Reduction of costs associated with occupational and nonoccupational disability is a major, though certainly not the only, reason for an employer to move to IDM. One of the questions most frequently asked by employers considering IDM is, "How much will it save?" The response from the consultant or service provider is the predictable, "How much are you spending now?" There almost always ensues a lengthy pause at this point because, for most employers, this is an extremely difficult question to answer.

A method for determining true total costs is discussed in Chapter 8; yet, it is important for employers to understand that those costs are not fixed. They are dynamic and driven by factors, many of which, if recognized, are controllable. A new program–however elaborate and sophisticated–will not achieve the desired result unless underlying workplace problems are recognized and corrected.

In the management of occupational and nonoccupational disabilities there are conditions and circumstances that, directly or indirectly, impact adversely on costs. These major cost drivers include:

- ◆ Workplace culture and environment
- ◆ Other workplace issues
- ◆ Medical provider behavior
- ◆ New causes of disability
- ◆ Aging of the workforce

Chapter 3

Understanding Key Drivers of Disability Costs and Their Impact on Productivity

by Janet R. Douglas,
Bruce L. Douglas and
John W. Stimson

- ◆ Benefit plan design
- ◆ Unmanaged absence
- ◆ Inefficient claims administration.

One of the benefits of an IDM program is its ability to reduce the effects of these cost drivers.

Workplace Culture and Environment

Recognizing that the work environment and the way employees are treated are direct drivers of disability costs often requires a major shift in thinking on the part of management. Modern management theory aims at increasing productivity, which results in increased share value. It does not usually consider the impact that major changes have on the physical and psychological well-being of employees. For example, downsizing has been seen as a universal solution to industry woes. Downsizing, however, is a major driver of occupational and nonoccupational disability costs. Those who receive a pink slip have a right to be stressed, but what about those who are left behind? What about those who have to deliver the news? Is there recognition or concern that these people's health is being jeopardized? Typically not.

Another seldom recognized driver of disability costs is the over-worked supervisor. There is a management process that places the immediate supervisor in a pivotally important role with respect to managing employees' injuries and illnesses. The supervisor, however, is often the most overworked, poorly trained and conflicted individual in the workplace. Supervisors participating in focus groups repeatedly say that managing workers' compensation and disability, particularly return to work, is the most unpleasant part of their job because they feel they have neither the knowledge nor the tools to handle it. No wonder the paperwork doesn't get turned in and decisions about return to work are received as arbitrary and capricious.

Certainly there is no substitute for personal contact between employees and supervisors, but should the supervisor really be the front-line disability manager? Probably not. An effective IDM program will place disability management in the hands of trained professionals who will make sure that supervisors have all the information they need to run their operations.

Other variables that drive disability include idiosyncrasies of the worker–reaction to illness, to injury, to pain and to prevention techniques–and the culture of the workplace, which is a demonstration of the values and priorities the company places on such matters as safety, prevention, early intervention, return to work, the older employee and, above all, interpersonal relationships.

In a unionized environment, the relationship between management and the union is often fundamental to the cultural stability of the workplace, and a subject that is very sensitive to workplace culture and union relationship is return to work. Most companies–whether unionized or not–will say they have a return-to-work policy, yet they are often hard pressed to produce a written document on the subject. (Usually return to work applies only to workers' compensation, and nonoccupational disability remains unmanaged.) They are even less able to demonstrate that all managers and supervisors understand and enforce the policy consistently. Inevitably, it comes down to the workplace culture in each work unit, which has everything to do with the relationships between the worker, the supervisor and the union steward.

A worker's ability to return to work from a disability is often determined by the personal bias of the immediate supervisor and, not infrequently, by the perceived strength or weakness of the union representative. The workplace culture often encourages staying off work rather than returning to work as quickly as possible. For IDM to succeed, these issues must be addressed.

Another unfortunate reality is the frequent use, by both workers and supervisors, of disability as an "escape hatch" to avoid facing performance issues and/or disciplinary action, because there is no strong, proactive support to deal appropriately with performance problems in the workplace.

An informal workplace culture also tends to encourage people to use disability time to save their vacation time or to receive more days off (when vacation and personal time have already been used).

Finally, "cashing in" on disability benefits is seen as a legal way to get one's "fair share" from the company if there is unrest in the workplace. This applies to downsizing, layoffs, mergers and acquisitions, and plant/ office closings, as well as to personal issues of job dissatisfaction, personality conflicts with management and burnout.

To be successful, IDM requires changing the culture or environment within the company. Since such changes may take years, involvement of senior management is critical. IDM must be discussed with union representatives so they understand the potential benefits of such changes in the disability management program, both in lowering costs and improving quality of services. Whenever possible, a union representative should be included as integration policies are formulated. Experience with IDM has shown that unions are, in fact, great supporters once they realize that employee satisfaction increases with more efficient and equitable administration of benefits and programs.

Other Workplace Issues

Other issues within the workplace that drive up costs include:

◆ Conflict between occupational and nonoccupational policies and processes with respect to time off and return to work

◆ Lack of recognition and rewards for good behavior (e.g., staying at work or returning to work early)

◆ Lack of punishment for bad behavior (e.g., taking unnecessary time off or failing to return to work as soon as possible)

◆ Failure to purchase health, workers' compensation and disability management services according to the same standards of quality and efficiency that employers use in their purchase of other business supplies (such as spare parts and raw materials)

◆ Underlying psychosocial issues: There has been significant research done by Michael Scofield[1] and others that shows that psychosocial factors play a key role in extending disability duration. It has been shown that the severity of an illness or injury actually plays only a minor role in determining how long an individual will stay away from work. Instead, high on the list of variables that determine duration of disability is an employee's relationship with the immediate supervisor. When the relationship is poor, there is a real disincentive for an employee to return to work. Other factors that affect ability or willingness to stay at work or return to work–such as medical provider behavior and new causes–are discussed below.

Medical Provider Behavior

Disability management is typically considered by physicians and others to be the purview of a few select medical specialties. Physiatrists, orthopedic surgeons, neurosurgeons and neurologists are those most commonly associated with rehabilitation, restoration of function and return to work. They receive some degree of training in disability management and usually have a reasonably good understanding of the consequences of time lost from work for both employer and employee.

The vast majority of medical practitioners, however, receive no training in disability management whatsoever. This includes general practitioners, emergency physicians, internists and many others who, on a daily basis, treat individuals absent from work as a result of an injury or illness–serious or trivial. A physician will usually be able to make an educated and accurate guess as to the costs of a procedure, a hospital stay, a lab test or an x-ray but has no idea of the cost of a lost workday to his patient's employer. There is a tendency, therefore, to look at time off as a harmless, inexpensive commodity to be dispensed freely. A physician, lacking specific knowledge of the physical or emotional requirements of a patient's job, often asks the patient if he or she is ready to return to work, thereby putting the patient (employee) in the driver's seat. There are times, especially in an environment of tightly managed care, when time off may be used as a substitute for or a delay of a more costly form of investigation or treatment. While not intended to cheat, steal or deprive the patient of necessary care, these expediencies–aimed at controlling some costs–often result in increasing others.

There are other factors that may inadvertently cause physicians to act as cost drivers. One important factor is the much ballyhooed and, sometimes overprotected, doctor-patient relationship. Doctors for the most part are very good people; they like to do good and they like to be liked. They do not like to be put in the position of making an unpopular decision that may cause a patient to become angry. They especially do not like to be put in a position that may make a patient angry enough to seek care elsewhere–or worse yet, sue!

For most physicians, determining when an individual is ready to resume working is usually an arbitrary decision made in the face of complex and often conflicting information and without benefit of objectivity. It is all too often left to the patient/employee to determine how long the disability should last. This is slowly changing as the use of disability duration guidelines, such as *The Medical Disability Advisor* by Presley Reed, are providing physicians with tools to assist in disability management.

New Causes of Disability

Major insurers of long-term disability report their longest categories of diagnoses are mental/nervous and musculoskeletal. The latter part of the 20th century has seen the emergence of a number of conditions that are extremely hard to manage and often result in lengthy absence from work and are, consequently, major drivers of cost. These include chronic fatigue syndrome, repetitive stress disorders, stress and depression. They all have the following characteristics in common: they have both physical and psychological symptoms, they are hard to diagnose early and they are chronic in nature. In other words, they tend not to progress from acute onset through complete recovery within a specified time frame. Because these conditions are poorly understood and symptoms are often perceived as subjective, individuals tend to be kept out of the workplace either by their physicians or at their own volition. Removal from the structure and activity of work will often cause the condition to deteriorate–the opposite of the desired outcome!

No other "medical" condition impacts as insidiously, as profoundly, and as broadly on the human body as stress. Webster's dictionary defines *stress* as "strain; pressure; esp. force exerted upon a body that tends to strain or deform its shape." While the implication of that definition is physical in nature, stress, in the psychosocial sense, does much the same thing to the human body and the human mind. Within the workplace, some stress encourages competition and can lead to increased productivity. But while a little stress may be a good thing, no stress or too much stress is not.

In a 1991 survey, 46% of workers reported their jobs were in the "highly stressful" category. Seventeen percent of those workers said stress was enough to make them miss at least one day of work during the year.[2]

Almost any medical problem can have a stress component; but some are much more clearly classifiable as stress-related diseases than others (e.g., depression, tension headaches, migraine headaches, insomnia, alcoholism, drug addiction, asthma, ulcers, skin rashes, hypertension, angina, gastritis, chronic fatigue, and fibromyalgia). Constant stress can also generate anxiety and anger, bring about dependencies on food, alcohol, tranquilizers, stimulants, analgesics, tobacco and other drugs, and cause tension with co-workers, which may lead to accidents or violence.

Employers that are undergoing changes, particularly financially challenging ones, should be aware of the stress placed upon their employees and recognize there is an associated increase in cost and decrease in productivity.

The Aging Workforce

Aging is often a factor in the job performance of employees and an inherent driver of disability duration and cost. Chronological age is essentially irrelevant to individual physical, cognitive and psychosocial behavior; however, as a group, the effects of aging on workers, particularly their abilities to recover from illness and injury, lead to increased costs. In addition, the older the group, the greater the incidence of various types of pathological conditions (e.g., arthritis, cardiovascular disease, cancer, diabetes, and sight and hearing disorders).

Even though older workers tend to be more careful and less frequently

Exhibit 3A

WORK DAYS LOST FOLLOWING INJURIES OR ILLNESSES[3]

Age	Median Lost Days
14-15	2
16-19	4
20-24	4
25-34	5
35-44	6
45-54	8
55-65	9
65+	10

injured, when they do get injured, they take longer to heal. (See Exhibit 3A.)

For the older employee, organic disease (e.g., high blood pressure) and comorbidities frequently lengthen recovery time and delay return to work. And it is often impossible to separate preexisting nonoccupational medical problems from workplace injuries and illnesses. By handling both workplace and nonoccupational disabilities, IDM reduces the time spent determining the root of an injury or illness and addresses getting the older employee back to work more efficiently.

The aging workforce's effects on costs may be diminished through prevention programs as well. A physically and emotionally fit older worker is less likely to have accidents, less likely to get sick and more likely to recuperate and return to work quickly than one who does not take good care of himself. It is becoming increasingly important, then, for companies to develop programs to assist aging workers in remaining healthy.

None of this happens by chance. Company culture should foster prevention among its employees. If the company provides appropriate safety and prevention programs, it demonstrates sensitivity to its employees' needs, which in turn saves money, improves morale and enhances productivity.

Benefit Plan Design

A strong argument for consideration of IDM is found frequently within the design of employee benefit plans. Historically, disability benefit plans have their origins in paternalism. Employers, often motivated by a sincere desire to protect employees and to reward them for their loyalty and steadfastness, provided compensation in times of illness and injury. Many of these plans preceded, accompanied or followed shortly after statutory disability benefits such as Social Security and workers' compensation. In other cases employers, especially following World War II and continuing to the present, were determined to get and keep a competitive edge in their respective industries. This led to the establishment of what was considered to be "gold-standard" disability plans. The objectives were to promote recruitment and ensure retention and, in some instances, to prevent the entry of organized labor into the workplace.

Regardless of the historical motivations of employers, the end result is that disability benefit plans now serve as major disability cost drivers in and of themselves. All too often salary replacement benefits are at best "disincentives" to early return to work and, at worst, encouragement for disability. Evidence of these unfortunate and costly events may be found in both the private and public sectors.

Employers that supplement state-regulated, tax-free workers' compensation indemnity payments (66⅔% of annual pay) to bring pay to 100% actually end up with employees whose income surpasses their on-the-job, take-home pay. Another example of this type of financial disincentive is found in the public sector where an employees' participation in state-established public safety and fire pension plans automatically ensures a full year of full-time pay for a medical disability. Why return to work on restricted duty when income rises, vacation time accrues and benefits continue to be accessible while at home?

Disability benefit waiting periods often encourage employees to be absent by compensating them at 100% pay when they are off work the full waiting period (usually seven days) before short-term disability coverage begins. While acute health care problems and emergency situations may seem to justify this practice, many short-term disability claims (such as elective surgeries and medical treatments) are scheduled events and, thus, do not warrant a week's absence prior to health care services.

Employers that are looking into the costs of disability benefits should also consider the financial impact of a nontraditional disability benefit—sick days. Most commonly found in the area of employee benefits having to do with paid time off, which includes vacation and holiday time, sick days' potential as a disability cost driver lies in the unpredictability of the use of the benefit. The practice of providing employees annually with anywhere from one to three weeks pay for being sick, all on an unscheduled basis, motivates employees to use or lose the benefit. The existence of this largely uncontrolled benefit suggests it is an important cost driver.

Inefficient Claims Administration

Increased efficiency in claims administration is an important factor in IDM. Several aspects of the existing silo-based structure are known to drive up costs. These are:
◆ A disjointed and overlapping administration process
◆ Unnecessarily high staffing levels
◆ Redundant documentation.

Administration Process

A major obstacle to controlling the administrative costs of occupational and nonoccupational disability management exists when the third-party administrator, the insurance company and the employer's workers' compensation or benefits representative play conflicting or overlapping roles (as they often do in a system that differentiates illnesses and injuries primarily by whether they occur on or off the job). In this disjointed system the worker, the claims manager, the provider and even the care manager may have no clear idea of appropriate communication channels or responsibilities, and the injured or ill employee often becomes confused and frustrated, unaware to whom he is responsible and from whom he is receiving his benefits.

The ensuing confusion and frustration translate directly into a "noise factor." The higher the level of frustration with the benefit delivery system, the louder the noise factor, sometimes reaching all the way up to top management. Controlling this noise factor can become expensive. The louder the noise, the more customer service is needed; the more customer service is needed, the higher administrative costs are going to climb.

Asking the following questions about the administrative process should pinpoint areas for scrutiny:
◆ How many times does the claim change hands from beginning to end?

- How many different signoffs are required during the life of a claim?
- How paper dependent is the process?
- Is every claim treated exactly the same in the workflow? If not, how do they differ?
- How many reports are generated each week? Month? To whom are these reports sent?
- How many modifications have been made to the disability plan(s) due to union negotiations?
- On average, how long does it take an appeal to move through the process from beginning to end?
- How often do human resources, the law department, labor relations, and/or the medical department get involved in claims activity?
- How much settlement authority resides with each level of adjudication?
- To what degree are medical records, reports and claims documents shared among all the interested parties?

Staffing Levels

Staffing is another critical administrative cost driver. And there is more involved here than merely counting the number of bodies. What is the accepted caseload for an adjuster compared to the degree of risk management expected? What is the ratio of support staff to adjusters? What is the ratio of supervisors to adjusters? How many specialists (e.g., customer service representatives, return-to-work specialists and litigation managers) support the claims management function? How are vacations covered? How is work managed when someone is out ill? How is training given while maintaining the workflow?

Documentation

Finally, what level of documentation is expected to verify a disability? What percentage of this documentation is received with one request? Two? Three or more? How often is a determination made based on the original documentation? How often is additional documentation requested? How often do other parties get involved in securing documentation or reviewing documentation? How often are independent medical examinations (IMEs) required?

IDM minimizes these administrative cost drivers by eliminating confusion (through, for example, common intake of claims information), by streamlining the claims handling process, and by reducing redundant staffing and unnecessary documentation.

Unmanaged Absence

Physical absence from work carries with it numerous direct and indirect costs. Employers and claim administrators are well aware of the *paid* and *reserved* columns commonly found on a loss run. What is often overlooked, however, are the indirect costs associated with absence. For instance, an employee who is away from work creates a void in the productivity of the position, the department, the division and the company as a whole. In order to fill that void, employers may be forced to hire temporary help or shuffle the burden onto existing co-workers. While temporary help is fairly easy to monitor and quantify in terms of dollars paid out, it carries with it questions concerning the productivity level of the temp and the quality of work produced. The disparity between the regular employee and the temp can be further increased based on the difficulty level of the position and the number of years of experience the employee has both in that type of position and with the company. (See Exhibit 3B.)

The use of existing workers to fill the void left by a disability-related absence carries with it a number of different problems that need to be considered and addressed. First, there is the cost of overtime compensation for those positions paid on an hourly basis. This increases costs by between 1.5 and 2 times the normal hourly rate for the same amount of hours that would have been covered by the disabled employee. Issues of quality and levels of productivity arise as they did with temporary employees. How much can one person work in one day at a sustained level of productivity? The answer varies, but the point is there are thresholds as to the number of hours worked per day, number of days worked per week, and the number of consecutive workdays with excessive overtime that an individual can *effectively* work. While the lure of extra money (earned through overtime) can produce enthusiasm in many employees, that enthusiasm is often tempered, as the situation is repeated, by the pressure of more responsibility and the disruption overtime can bring to an employee's environment outside of the workplace.

The nonhourly employee may relieve the employer from the added costs of overtime, but the issues of quality and level of productivity remain. In some industries and with some positions, the difficulties of replacement can also be enhanced with the nonhourly employee, thereby making replacement a more time-consuming and cost-increasing issue.

Exhibit 3B

CONCERNS RAISED BY WORKER ABSENCE

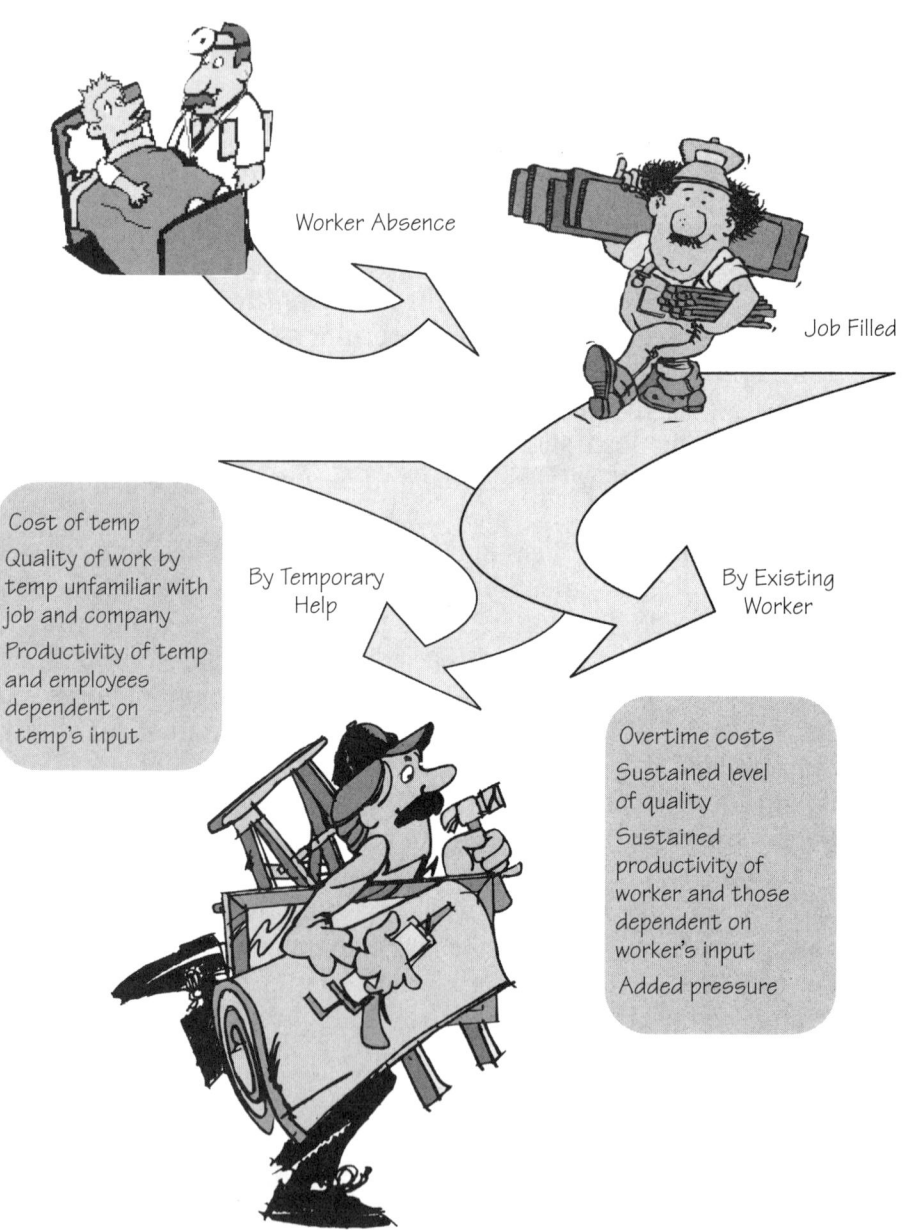

Worker Absence

Job Filled

By Temporary Help

By Existing Worker

Cost of temp

Quality of work by temp unfamiliar with job and company

Productivity of temp and employees dependent on temp's input

Overtime costs

Sustained level of quality

Sustained productivity of worker and those dependent on worker's input

Added pressure

Regardless of the type of employee, absence from work is expensive for the employer. The combination of direct costs and indirect costs associated with the actual absence makes this the single most costly variable in the total cost of disability equation. Thus, it is not surprising that employers look first to absence/lost time as a source of potentially reducing disability costs.

Health-Related Productivity[4]

While this chapter has identified some of the major cost drivers inflicting employers when an employee is disabled, there remains the issue of how to measure, assess and intervene appropriately. The evaluation process is a program component that is often overlooked until someone or some group in an organization has to justify the use of a vendor, the existence of a program or the need to implement a program. Chapter 8 will detail how an evaluation of a program is conducted, but it is important to discuss the philosophical approach an employer should take in light of the cost drivers identified in this chapter.

Termed *health-related productivity* and defined as that portion of an organization's total output directly affected by individual and organizational health, the approach has evolved from much of the thinking behind IDM. The health-related productivity paradigm is a powerful way to analyze and understand the complex drivers and linkages that affect costs related to claims administration, workplace environment, and medical utilization and lost time. In addition, this paradigm enables an employer to measure the effectiveness of program alterations, thereby creating a comprehensive management system for an IDM program. To implement such a management system, however, requires a transformation in the way an employer typically gathers, stores and analyzes information.

Health-related productivity management is the link between the health of the individual employee, his organizational environment and the corporation's success through the application of information. All too often, the information gathered and used by employers is a static representation of past performance. In a health-related productivity approach, information is used proactively to maximize employee potential and performance resulting in an *optimal return* on investment for the organization with regard to both human resources and product or service profitability.

The process of developing a health-related productivity management model (depicted in Exhibit 3C) starts with identifying the key cost drivers of disability identified earlier in this chapter. Once identified and meas-

Exhibit 3C

HEALTH-RELATED PRODUCTIVITY MANAGEMENT

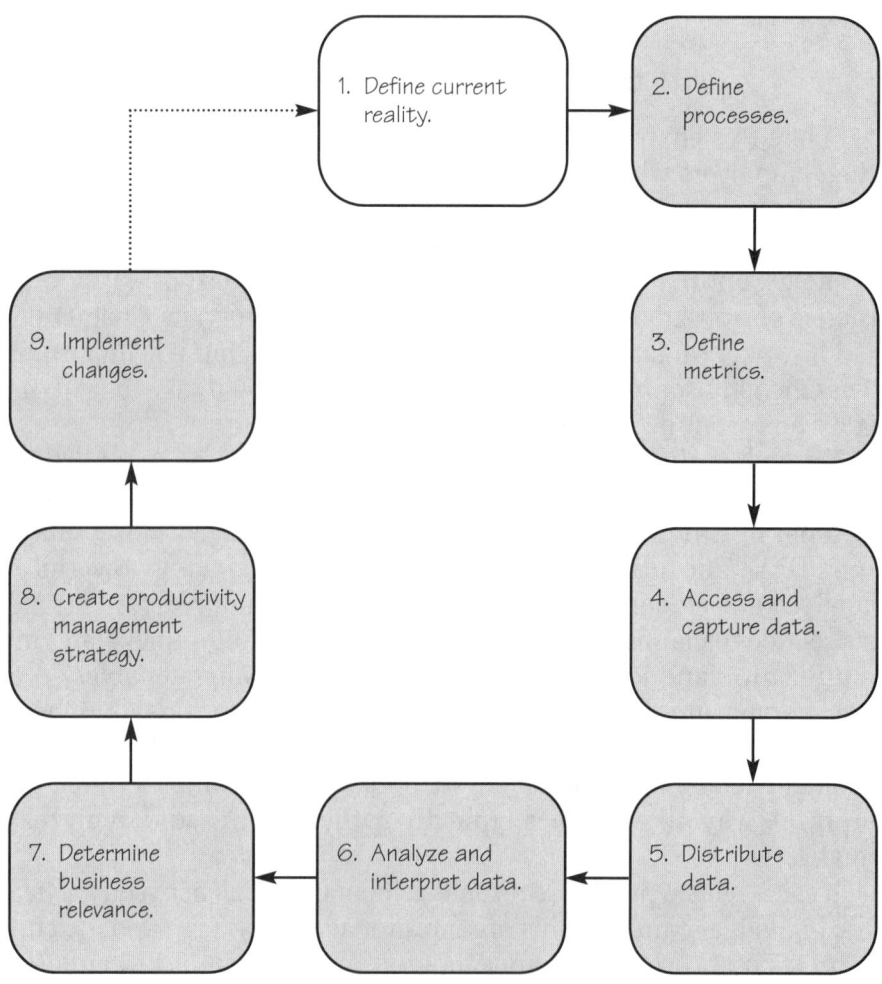

ured, the employer will have a clear picture of the *current reality* (Step 1) for the company and a baseline of information by which to measure interventions.

Step 2 is to *define the process* through which occupational and nonoccupational disability is managed. This includes vendor management and coordination as well as monitoring in-house programs such as safety and return to work.

Step 3 is to *define the metrics* that will be used to measure costs. Employers should begin with measures used to describe the current state but should not limit themselves to these. Rather, this provides the employer with the opportunity to expand on current measures in order to more accurately represent the costs and the cost drivers of disability.

The fourth step, *access and capture data,* is likely to involve the development of an integrated data system that colocates all the necessary data elements for analysis. As a substep, the employer may wish to develop or outsource a health management center that monitors the effectiveness of the claims handling process (regardless of whether it is in-house or outsourced) and coordinates the data and data needs of the health-related productivity management process. The cost benefit of outsourcing this part of the process is contingent upon the current data-capturing and analysis capabilities of the employer.

The fifth step, *distribute data,* will vary depending on the vendors involved. Reporting is the issue with an outsourced claims management process but is primarily an analysis issue if the program is self-administered. Using a vendor model, there are two issues that need to be addressed. First, report content and distribution timing are essential and must be worked out with any vendor. Unfortunately, they are often forgotten until the first report is received, which is often too late, since the time necessary to customize a reporting system can often takes months. These issues need to be addressed at the start of development for an integrated program rather than just prior to implementation or when the employer is ready to evaluate the program. Second, the sophisticated employer usually has both a need and a desire to conduct additional analysis of program data. Therefore, accessibility to vendor data is essential. A growing number of employers are demanding that their company experience be available through the Internet as a means to access, download and, in some instances, analyze data. While the paper report and disk transfer remains popular and is likely to continue for some time, the ability to access data through the Internet, or even a direct dial-up connection, is a sign to employers of an innovative vendor.

Next (Step 6), the *data needs to be analyzed* using a variety of statistical methods aimed at three areas, which:

- ◆ Describe the current state
- ◆ Identify year-to-year trends
- ◆ Build relational models between determining factors (e.g., cost drivers and interventions) and outcomes.

The analysis provides the employer with the information necessary to *determine the business relevance* (Step 7) of the relationships measured.

In so doing, the employer is able to look prospectively at what changes can be implemented to *create a health-related productivity management strategy* (Step 8). The goals of such a strategy focus both on the individual employee and the corporate structure of the company. For the employee, the strategy provides the opportunity to:

- Improve health and reduce risk factors
- Promote employee accountability for personal health
- Enhance employee self-image and self-worth
- Improve employee commitment and contribution to corporate success.

Similar considerations are given to the company, where the goals of a health-related productivity strategy attempt to:

- Identify and alter dysfunctional management and organizational environments
- Promote corporate accountability for organizational health
- Generate information and understanding that positively impact on growth, profitability and customer satisfaction.

Step 9 *implements the changes* that become current reality and bring an employer full circle.

Endnotes

1. Michael E. Scofield, "Development of the AT&T Health Audit for Measuring Organizational Health," *Occupational Medicine,* October 1990, pp. 755-788.

2. George J. Pfeiffer and Judith A. Webster, *Workcare: A Resource Guide for the Working Person* (Charlottesville, Va.: WorkCare Press, 1992), 184.

3. Bureau of Labor Statistics, U. S. Department of Labor, *Lost-Worktime Injuries and Illnesses: Characteristics and Resulting Time Away from Work, 1996,* ftp://146.4.23/pub/news.release/osh2.txt, April 23, 1998.

4. The term and information on *Health-Related Productivity* is contributed by Richard A. Lewis, M.B.A., and Edward L. Anderson, M.D., owners of Nucleus, LLC (Deerfield, Il. and Washington, D.C.), a company that specializes in optimizing workforce effectiveness.

E ach component of an integrated disability benefit program—medical, workers' compensation and disability (short- and long-term)—presents separate potential liabilities under federal, and sometimes state, law. The sophisticated services required to integrate these three effectively (including claims administration, tracking and payment, utilization review and case management, and the coordination of data among insurers, service companies and employers) add another layer of legal complexity.

This chapter will review the sources of these liabilities, show how they are expanding and summarize many tested techniques for minimizing the risk to employers (and managers individually).

Chapter 4

Legal Liability Under an IDM Program

by David L. Wolfe and Timothy J. Stanton

Historical Perspective

Court rulings in lawsuits over disability-related benefits traditionally have focused on employer denials of individual employee claims. In the traditional nonintegrated environment, employees generally have to make separate claims under two separate systems (medical or workers' compensation, and then disability) for a single illness or injury. This creates substantial administrative inefficiencies and great potential for inconsistency in processing and review standards and procedures. The result: high administrative costs, dissatisfaction for both employees and providers, and litigation.

By streamlining claims procedures, coordinating claims reviews and involving providers and other vendors, integrated disability programs can improve efficiency and cut costs. The potential, however, for significant legal liability continues.

Federal Versus State Law

Potential employer liability under integrated disability programs may result under federal or state law. Potential sources of liability under federal law include:

◆ Claims procedure rules for health plans subject to the Employee Retirement Income Security Act of 1974 (ERISA)
◆ Claims procedure rules for long-term disability plans subject to ERISA
◆ Unpaid leave requirements of the Family and Medical Leave Act of 1993 (FMLA)
◆ Health coverage continuation requirements of the Consolidated Omnibus Budget Reconciliation Act of 1985 (COBRA)
◆ Nondiscrimination rules of Section 510 of ERISA
◆ Employment provisions of the Americans with Disabilities Act of 1990 (ADA)
◆ Fiduciary and co-fiduciary responsibility provisions of ERISA for health and long-term disability plans
◆ Health coverage portability and nondiscrimination rules of the Health Insurance Portability and Accountability Act of 1996 (HIPAA)
◆ "Federal health care offense" rules of HIPAA
◆ Federal privacy rules including those in HIPAA and the ADA.

Potential sources of liability under state law include:

◆ Claims procedure rules that apply to short-term disability plans or payroll practices
◆ Claims procedure rules that apply to workers' compensation claims
◆ Contract law (in the case of breaches of third-party administrator [TPA] and other vendor contracts)
◆ Insurance laws and regulations
◆ Privacy laws
◆ TPA registration and licensing requirements.

When it was enacted in 1974, ERISA was viewed as a major protection of employee rights under most employer-sponsored health and welfare plans. In the last quarter century, however, numerous state laws have required employers (at least those with insured plans) to provide specific types or levels of coverage for employees. These laws go far beyond their federal counterpart in ERISA (which generally does not require employers to provide specific types or levels of coverage). The debate continues over how these state laws should fare under ERISA, which generally preempts state laws that relate to ERISA-governed plans.

Employers, in fact, have sometimes attempted to use the ERISA preemption provision as a shield to prevent them from becoming subject to more employee-protective state legislation. For many years, the strategy worked. Courts routinely ruled that employers were not subject to various state laws related to benefits. While a discussion of the history of ERISA preemption court decisions is beyond the scope of this chapter, it is important to note that courts have done an about face. Since a 1995 Supreme Court ruling,[1] in fact, courts may be said to have adopted a presumption *against* preemption, meaning that integrated disability programs may become subject to a broader array of state laws.

Practical Issues in Handling Contested Matters

When faced with a possible claim under ERISA or state law, plaintiffs often sue in state courts with a primary focus on their state law causes of action. The reasons for this are generally threefold.

First, most state laws provide for jury trials while ERISA does not (and conventional wisdom suggests that juries will provide for greater damage awards than judges would in a bench trial).

Second, damage awards are often higher under state laws than they would be under ERISA. (Punitive damages, for example, are generally not available under ERISA, but are under many state laws.) Moreover, ERISA generally requires the employer to pay only the level of benefits provided in the underlying plan document. State courts often adopt a standard more favorable to employees. Looking beyond the plan terms, state courts often consider items such as oral and written promises by an employer to provide higher levels of benefits than the plan itself contemplates.

A third important reason plaintiffs tend to file in state courts is federal courts applying ERISA often give greater deference to the initial administrative actions than do state courts. This difference results from the 1989 U.S. Supreme Court decision in *Firestone v. Bruch,*[2] which concluded that an ERISA administrative action will not be overturned unless the court determines the action to be "arbitrary and capricious" if the following two elements are present: (1) the plan reserves broad discretion to the fiduciary in question in undertaking the action; and (2) the action does not call into question an inherent internal conflict of interest. In state court proceedings, in contrast, the court will generally put itself into the shoes of the original decision maker and review all the facts underlying the action in question. Only if the action is deemed to be reasonable and appropriate will it be upheld.

Another tactical issue in resolving contested claims in an integrated disability program is whether to mandate binding arbitration of claims in lieu of litigation. Arbitration is generally considered quicker and less costly. However, its drawbacks may include less rigorous fact gathering before the proceeding takes place and arbitrators who are less experienced with integrated disability claims than judges might be.

Fiduciary Dimensions of Administrative Actions

Most lawsuits involving integrated disability programs will include claims alleging violations of fiduciary duties. This is an important tactic for plaintiffs because including fiduciary violations will instantly make the action important to the individuals named as defendants, thus increasing the likelihood of an early settlement on terms advantageous to the plaintiffs. Fiduciary claims are also becoming more prevalent as courts increasingly find for plaintiffs on such theories as failure of the fiduciaries to follow the terms of the underlying plan documents, failure to provide sufficient disclosures to plan participants, and failure to grant participants their right to a full and fair review due to conflicts of interest inherent in plan structure or administration.

Who Is a Fiduciary?

ERISA categorizes an employer's principal internal decision makers as *fiduciaries* because they have the ultimate discretionary authority in plan administration. A board of directors, an administrative committee assigned various strategic responsibilities under the plan and a plan administrator handling day-to-day administrative issues may all be fiduciaries at any one time. Fiduciary functions are also often delegated to TPAs and other external providers. Any such delegation should be accomplished in writing (see section on page 51 on drafting an administrative services agreement) so the chain of decision-making authority remains easy to identify. In the last analysis, however, ERISA imposes fiduciary status based on what a party does or is empowered to do, even in the absence of a written document spelling out that role. Some of the external administrative functions that may create fiduciary status in an integrated disability case include precertifications for medical procedures, level of care decisions, and claims processing and review.

Also affecting integrated disability programs are state laws that adopt fiduciary standards of conduct for parties with a legal responsibility for administering assets and liabilities on behalf of another party.

Fiduciary Obligations

The principal obligations of fiduciaries under ERISA health and long-term disability plans include:
- ◆ An obligation to discharge their duties for the exclusive benefit of plan participants and their beneficiaries
- ◆ An obligation to act prudently
- ◆ An obligation to follow the terms of the underlying plan document
- ◆ An obligation to avoid conflicts of interest in discharging their duties by not:
  - –Dealing with plan assets in the fiduciary's own interest or for the fiduciary's own account
  - –Acting on behalf of a party (or representing a party) whose interests are adverse to the interests of the plan or of its participants or beneficiaries or
  - –Receiving any consideration for the fiduciary's personal account from any party dealing with the plan in connection with any transaction involving plan assets.

Potential Sources of Fiduciary Liability Under IDM Programs

Fiduciary liability may be imposed in a variety of ways under an integrated disability program. For example, an employer's internal fiduciaries may be liable for imprudently retaining or selecting TPAs or other providers. (See section on Selecting Third-Party Administrators, page 50.) Fiduciaries assigned to make precertification or level-of-care decisions, or to process and review claims, may also be liable for imprudently handling those duties. In fact, according to the U.S. Department of Labor (DOL),[3] fiduciaries have a duty to consider quality of care when selecting providers to provide care under a health plan–an obligation that presumably would exist in an integrated disability program as well.

Courts have also questioned the very design of certain managed care systems with too much potential for inherent conflicts of interest. Examples include systems where an employer or TPA directly benefits when services to employees are denied or where cost savings otherwise are realized. Some courts have also ruled that an independent fiduciary may be required to resolve disputes involving such conflict situations.

In a somewhat analogous situation, when an affiliate of a health care provider gives discounts to those of its employees who choose to receive care from that health care provider, the potential for a *prohibited transaction* under ERISA exists based on the argument that the internal plan fiduciary acting on behalf of the employer is dealing with plan assets for its own account either directly or indirectly through the employer. Several years ago an employer received an individual prohibited transaction exemption[4] from the DOL under such a scenario. To obtain the exemption, the employer was willing to subject itself to the following restrictions:

◆ Participating employees were given a choice of provider (not just the health care provider affiliated with the employer).

◆ At least 50% of the health care providers offered were independent of the plan sponsor/employer.

◆ Fees were to be negotiated by an independent fiduciary.

◆ The providers were also selected by the independent fiduciary.

While most employers have not gone nearly that far in ensuring employee choice of providers and independent fiduciary determinations, the exemption provides useful guidance of how at least one employer successfully protected itself from DOL scrutiny in the affiliated health care provider context. Obviously, the above conditions are rather onerous, and the DOL may approve less restrictive alternatives in the future.

Co-Fiduciary Liability

Due to the interaction of numerous providers in a "typical" integrated disability program, significant potential for co-fiduciary liability under ERISA also exists. Under ERISA, one fiduciary can be liable for another fiduciary's violations in the following situations:

◆ He participates knowingly in, or knowingly undertakes to conceal, a fiduciary breach of the other fiduciary, knowing that the breach exists.

◆ By failing to fulfill his own fiduciary duties, he enables the other party to commit the breach.

◆ He has knowledge of the other fiduciary's breach, unless he makes reasonable efforts to remedy the breach.

Fiduciary or Not?

Applying these standards becomes even more murky because it is often difficult to determine exactly which providers are acting as fiduciaries and which are providing only ministerial or advisory functions. For years, courts had held that ERISA permitted lawsuits against non-fiduciaries–such as recordkeepers to plans or other service providers–

if these nonfiduciaries "knowingly participated" in a fiduciary's breach of duty. In an important 1993 case,[5] the Supreme Court drew a bright line when it ruled that ERISA in fact does not authorize suits for money damages against nonfiduciaries. This makes it even more important to be able to determine who is a fiduciary and who is not.

Misrepresentation

One recent U.S. Supreme Court decision[6] raises even more thorny fiduciary issues. In that case, the court upheld employee claims that a legal right of action exists against plan fiduciaries where the fiduciaries have engaged in deliberate misrepresentations that harmed the employees. The conduct of the fiduciaries in question was so egregious that the equitable relief afforded to the employees was a just result. Employers, however, are left with substantial uncertainty whether similar liability will be imposed in future cases based on nondisclosure of certain relevant information to employees (rather than more active misrepresentations as to material facts). Even more troubling to employers and fiduciaries could be an extension of these principles to situations where the fiduciaries provide all necessary general informative materials to employees under ERISA, but fail to provide individualized materials to cover all issues relevant to a specific covered employee.

Duty to Disclose

In a somewhat similar vein of cases, courts have generally ruled that fiduciaries have a duty to disclose the existence of a plan to employees not only when the plan is adopted, but also when it is under "serious consideration." This earlier disclosure presumably better enables employees to make ongoing employment decisions and possibly avail themselves of benefits they would otherwise miss. Of course, it is difficult under this standard to know exactly when initial disclosure is required.

Many other cases consider the fiduciary and disclosure implications of various employer actions that may be relevant to managed disability programs. For example, a recent U.S. Supreme Court decision[7] confirmed that an employer may amend or terminate an ERISA plan without fiduciary implications or judicial second-guessing (the premise being that the decision of whether to provide the benefits or what level or types of benefits to provide is a business decision of the employer). Other cases analyze disclosure of individual eligibility for benefits, financial incentives built into a managed care plan and information important in the specific circumstances of some participants.

Selecting Third-Party Administrators

TPAs play a pivotal role in servicing an effective integrated disability program. Care should be taken at the outset to identify the range of required services and to identify which TPAs offer the best package of such services. An employer's internal fiduciaries responsible for making the discretionary medical, disability and workers' compensation decisions need to take this TPA selection process seriously. As part of their due diligence, the following questions should be asked, answered and documented:

- ◆ Does the TPA offer appropriate claims administration, tracking and payment services, which satisfy the existing legal standards for such services and the new, much tighter DOL claims-processing deadlines that may be imposed?[8]
- ◆ Are relevant state insurance law requirements monitored and incorporated appropriately into the program?
- ◆ What information systems and software does the TPA utilize?
- ◆ What utilization review and case management services are available and how successful have they been for other clients of the TPA?
- ◆ What procedures are in place to collect and analyze information from insurers, providers and the employer?
- ◆ How experienced are the TPA personnel who will be handling the account? How long have they been with the TPA?
- ◆ How long has the TPA been providing these services and what is its general track record in doing so (with possible references from satisfied clients)?
- ◆ What data confidentiality protections does the TPA utilize?
- ◆ How does the TPA coordinate various legal standards such as the COBRA health care continuation requirements, state workers' compensation rules, the ADA employment rules and the FMLA unpaid leave rules?
- ◆ Is the TPA willing to enter into a reasonable and detailed services contract?
- ◆ What cost-related performance guarantees will the TPA provide?

Protecting the Employer and Internal Fiduciaries From Liability

Employers and internal fiduciaries can take a number of steps to reduce their liability exposure in administering integrated disability programs. These steps include the following:

- ◆ Establish written procedures allocating responsibilities for administrative functions and dissemination of information among the employer, the TPA and other providers.

◆ Confirm periodically that these written procedures accurately reflect how the program is run.

◆ Determine which administrative functions are fiduciary in nature.

◆ Periodically review all participant disclosures (such as ERISA-mandated summary plan descriptions and summaries of material modifications) for consistency with actual plan terms and ongoing plan administrative practices.

◆ Maintain written administrative services contracts reflecting the current relationship with all administrative services providers.

◆ Maintain appropriate levels of fiduciary liability insurance to protect internal fiduciaries.

◆ Ensure the continuing existence and enforceability of indemnification protections from external service providers for the benefit of internal fiduciaries.

Drafting a Services Agreement to Minimize Liability

A services agreement should be completed and executed by both the employer and TPA before the TPA's services begin. This agreement should:

◆ Identify as precisely as possible the scope of services to be provided by the TPA.

◆ Specify the initial term of the agreement and any provision for its automatic renewal in the absence of written objections by either party.

◆ List the fees for all services and explain how they can be modified.

◆ Set TPA performance standards and penalties for failing to meet them (including the measurement period for the service standards, the method for calculating whether the standard is attained, and how the penalty is to be calculated).

◆ Describe how claims under the contract are to be resolved (possibly including an arbitration clause).

◆ Specify which state's law will govern enforcement and interpretation of the contract.

◆ Detail whether and how a party may assign its rights or duties to another party (including possible automatic successorship in cases of reorganization or sale of the TPA business).

◆ Set detailed rules for maintaining confidentiality of the data the TPA obtains in performing its services and the privacy of employee medical information as required by relevant state and federal laws.(For more on the subject, see "Privacy Concerns" on page 55.)

◆ Identify who owns the information systems and software used to administer the program and how the employer obtains access to them when the contract is terminated.

◆ Outline the TPA's disaster plan for recovering data and administering its systems in the event of emergencies.

◆ Specify the TPA's record retention policy and that policy's compliance with relevant legal requirements.

◆ Clarify how the contract can be amended by mutual written consent of the parties and how it can be terminated upon a material breach.

◆ Allocate legal liability between the parties and indemnify the aggrieved party when it is sued over the other party's performance of its duties. The misconduct standard could be measured by any one or more of the following (in general order from least to most egregious behavior): negligence, gross negligence, recklessness, willful misconduct and bad faith. The indemnification provision should identify all protected parties (the aggrieved party and its current and former officers, directors, employees, agents, etc.) and any limits on how much the aggrieved parties can recover from the party engaging in the specified types of misconduct. The provision should set a time limit that extends as far as, or beyond, the relevant statute of limitations period.

◆ Protect the employer appropriately from the Year 2000 software problems caused by the TPA's internal systems or external systems interacting with the TPA's systems. These protections may include representations of system compliance or at least ongoing reporting by the TPA of its due diligence efforts to ensure compliance (including questionnaires to its own service providers and external system interfaces about their own compliance initiatives).

FMLA, ADA and Workers' Compensation

Integrated disability programs must carefully navigate among the varying substantive requirements, definitions and covered employer rules of the Family and Medical Leave Act(FMLA), the employment provisions of the Americans with Disabilities Act (ADA) and relevant state workers' compensation statutes. An overview of how these rules sometimes differ and sometimes overlap follows.

FMLA

FMLA covers employers with more than 50 employees within 75 miles of the applicable worksite. It protects employees with at least one year of service who are employed for at least 1,250 hours on an annual basis. It requires that such employees be given up to 12 weeks of unpaid leave in any 12-month period due to birth of a child, placement of a child for adoption or foster care or "serious health conditions" of the employee, or his or her spouse, child or parent. It also provides for reinstatement rights at the end of the leave (to the same or an equivalent position) and continuation of employee benefits (including health benefits) for the duration of the leave.

Under FMLA it is irrelevant whether the leave would constitute a significant hardship for the employer or whether the employer would be willing to offer reasonable accommodations in lieu of the leave. It is also irrelevant that the employee may not be able to work at the end of the leave, although if the employee cannot perform the essential duties of the employee's original job after the leave, FMLA does not require that the employee be reinstated to his or her original job or to any different job. An employer may also require an employee to exhaust paid leave before taking unpaid FMLA leave.

ADA

ADA protects qualified employees and job applicants who have disabilities. Rather than deny such people employment opportunities, an employer is required to make "reasonable accommodations" to their mental or physical impairments. To fall within the ADA protections an employee must be able to perform the essential functions of his or her job with or without the employer's reasonable accommodations. If leave is granted under ADA and thereafter the employee cannot perform the essential duties of his or her job, the employer must make reasonable accommodations, such as modifying the job, transferring the employee to a different position or extending time off. Moreover, according to the Equal Employment Opportunity Commission, an employee may qualify under ADA even if the employee has applied for Social Security disability benefits. The Supreme Court has agreed to resolve this question.

Workers' Compensation

All 50 states have enacted laws to provide four general types of benefits for on-the-job injuries (and sometimes occupational diseases): medical care, rehabilitative care, death benefits and income replacement for temporary or permanent disabilities. Most states require employers to offer these benefits, so state laws will be an important consideration in any integrated disability program. By law, workers' compensation benefits are to be a workers' "exclusive remedy" for an on-the-job injury; that is, no damages may be sought in a civil suit against the employer.

To reduce personnel costs and to encourage employees to return to work sooner, employers often assign employees on workers' compensation leave to a light duty job. Under state law an employer may generally reduce benefits for an injured employee who rejects such a light duty assignment. Such an employee may also generally be terminated, although in either case the employee would still be eligible for any applicable FMLA protections (i.e., unpaid leave and benefit continuation during the leave). Time spent on light duty does not count as FMLA leave, and, although an employer can reduce workers' compensation benefits, it cannot require an employee to return from FMLA leave to take a light duty job. Note that light duty is not required by ADA unless as a reasonable accommodation.

HIPAA

The Health Insurance Portability and Accountability Act (HIPAA) added new benefit portability rules to the medical benefit portion of an integrated disability program. This was done primarily by prohibiting employer health plans from discriminating in eligibility, enrollment or cost based on health status, and by placing important restrictions on the use of preexisting condition exclusions. For example, the exclusions may now apply only for up to 12 months, and any exclusion period must be reduced by the period that an employee had coverage immediately before enrolling, usually with another employer plan. HIPAA also made several technical changes to the COBRA continuation coverage rules, two of which are relevant to integrated disability programs:

1. An individual may be eligible for the 11-month disability extension (on top of the standard 18 months of coverage) if he was disabled at the time he qualified for COBRA or becomes so during the first 60 days of coverage.
2. When one dependent or employee is entitled to this disability extension, so are all other covered family members.

HIPAA also created a "federal health care offense" effective as of January 1, 1997 for such actions as knowingly obtaining money from a private employer-sponsored health plan under false pretenses. An example of such an offense might be the improper health coverage of a boyfriend or girlfriend of an employee, or coverage for an ineligible outside director of the employer. This offense is punishable by penalties, fines and possible imprisonment.

In addition, HIPAA will attempt to standardize electronic health data beginning in February 2000. This will be accomplished through standardized employer identifier codes, provider identifier codes and individual covered participant identifier codes. The latter have proven to be particularly problematic and have raised acute privacy concerns that have been the subject of recent governmental hearings. The Clinton administration has recently imposed a moratorium on the issuance of such individual codes.

Privacy Concerns

Simplifying health plan administration—by using, for example, standard electronic codes—may add fuel to the fire of concern over medical records' confidentiality. Even before some rules ordered by HIPAA are to take effect, a number of states enacted laws to protect patient confidentiality. Congress recently considered, though did not pass, several medical privacy rights bills. HIPAA requires Congress to enact such legislation by August 1999, or the Department of Health and Human Services will enact privacy regulations.

Guaranteeing patient privacy presents special problems for administrators of integrated disability programs. Extensive amounts of data, all centrally stored and managed, are required to administer the programs day to day and to gauge their long-term effectiveness. This data can be used for a number of purposes and is often widely shared among employers, outside administrative services firms and health care providers (for case management, for example). The more parties and computer systems involved, and the greater the amounts of data they handle, the greater the risk of a breach of network security.

A recent Wisconsin case[9] focuses on the relationship between workers' compensation legislation and state privacy protections. In that case the court upheld the privacy rights of a former employee under state law. Commentators have suggested that such a result threatens the integrity of the exclusive remedy doctrine.

Summary

Potential liabilities are constantly expanding and pose a real threat to the financial integrity of an integrated disability program. However, many tested techniques can minimize the risk of such liability for any careful employer.

Endnotes

1. *New York State Conference of Blue Cross & Blue Shield Plans v. Travelers Ins. Co.*, 115 S. Ct. 1671 (1995).

2. 489 U.S. 101 (1989).

3. The letter was issued February 19, 1998 to the Service Employees' International Union. No identifying number was included in the original.

4. PTE 93-62.

5. *Mertens v. Hewitt Assocs.*, 113 S. Ct. 2063 (1993).

6. *Varity Corp. v. Howe*, 116 S. Ct. 1065 (1996).

7. *Lockheed v. Spink*, 116 S. Ct. 1783 (1996).

8. The DOL has proposed general deadlines of 72 hours to process an "urgent care" claim and 15 days for other claims. 63 Fcd. Reg. 48390.

9. *Marino v. Arandell*, 1 F.Supp.2d 947 (E.D. Wis., 1998).

Section III

The IDM Process

Why Integrate?

Within the robust American economy of the past few years, many companies have improved their profits dramatically; yet margins continue to be squeezed. While customer demands, required quality investments and low unemployment all affect margins, the major threat is increased competition. In most industries, multiple companies compete in the same market, and this competition is increasingly global, with many foreign companies enjoying less-regulated business environments and lower operating costs than American companies.

Cognizant of the need to improve profits and be competitive, wise American managers are continually looking for ways to control costs. In a low unemployment economy this cannot be done at the expense of employees. Within this climate, disability—an area that impacts both profits and employees—is receiving close scrutiny.

For most American companies, disability (especially nonoccupational) has been a relatively uncontrolled area. Recent reports suggest that total disability costs can be in the range of 6% to 20% of total payroll costs.[1] Further, the DOL reports that total disability costs are rising at about 8% per year for the average American company.[2] This makes disability (already the most expensive human resource cost behind payroll) the fastest

Chapter 5

Assessing a Company's Readiness for IDM

by John S. O'Connor II

growing personnel expense. To be, or to remain, competitive in a tough global economy, American companies must get a handle on this last unmanaged personnel cost.

To accomplish this goal, many employers are investigating IDM. The IDM concept is simple and straightforward: process efficiencies and cost savings can be obtained by the aggressive management of a company's occupational and nonoccupational medical and disability benefits. The most efficient way to manage these benefit programs is to combine them under a single management system, which often leads to significant cost savings.

The benefits of IDM extend beyond process efficiency and cost savings. Effectively run IDM programs improve productivity by reducing lost time and enhancing employee morale. IDM's impact on productivity alone, although often overlooked, can be as important to the profitability of a company as reduced expense. Another important aspect of IDM programs is the collection of comprehensive absence, disability and medical care information that is critical for program evaluation and management. In addition, access to accurate event data for both occupational and nonoccupational illness and injuries is necessary for designing and implementing appropriate preventive strategies.

With the evidence strongly pointing to the benefits of IDM, why have companies been slow to integrate their occupational and nonoccupational disability programs?[3] Recent investigations supply some answers. In 1997, IntegraComp and Sedgwick conducted a study of the obstacles managers perceive as standing in the way of adopting integrated disability management.[4] This survey, which queried 500 risk managers and human resource managers from companies across the United States, revealed the following obstacles (listed in order of importance with percentage of respondents) to the implementation of IDM programs:

◆ Data system incompatibility (45.8%)
◆ Lack of vendor experience (43.2%)
◆ Lack of management commitment (40.4%)
◆ Implementation costs (37.7%)
◆ Benefit to the organization (33.4%)
◆ Internal turf issues (31.1%).

IntegraComp's findings also support the contention that many companies do not have a good understanding of IDM or what is available in the IDM marketplace.

The same is true of brokers and consultants who influence company management changes. In a survey of brokers conducted by Alexander and

Alexander in 1997[5] one-third indicated they did not understand IDM, and 86% felt there were few proven IDM products available.

Adoption of IDM is slowed further by companies that understand IDM but lack the leadership necessary to overcome the natural bureaucratic reluctance to change. Often at issue is an organizational structure that gives the chief financial officer responsibility for occupational disability (workers' compensation) and charges human resources with the nonoccupational disability benefits function (short- and long-term disability programs). Such a separation in programs is seldom justified from a management perspective, yet frequently creates a "turf" issue that is difficult to overcome without visionary leadership.

Armed with accurate information and farsighted leadership, however, companies can conquer the obstacles and implement an IDM program that is a win-win proposition.

IDM Advantages

How can a company determine if it is a good candidate for IDM and whether IDM can deliver its reported process improvements and savings? Although there is no definitive process for determining whether or not a company should move to IDM, there are three main areas where an IDM program can help a company: increased process efficiency, reduced disability costs and improved availability of disability data.[6] A company should consider how much it might benefit from each of these interrelated areas, which are discussed below.

Process Efficiency

A major argument for IDM is that it provides improved administrative efficiencies. It is hard to justify from a business perspective using two benefit delivery systems (one for occupational injuries/illnesses and another for injuries/illnesses that take place away from the workplace) when the service and assistance each provides are essentially the same.

By moving to IDM a company gains several significant administrative advantages. A common claims notification process—where employees and/or supervisors can report any type of disability claim—makes access to promised benefits easier and faster. This eliminates the frequently expressed employee complaint, "It's a hassle to get the process to work correctly." Providing benefits and assistance when they are needed is an important step in improving employee morale, which by itself has far-ranging job implications. Additionally, with a single process and claims adjudication system there are often lower staff requirements. In some cases where staff members are cross-trained, individual adjusters handle both occupational and nonoccupational claims. In other IDM units a team approach is used. In either situation, any reduction in staff headcount should be done judiciously for it is often a sticking point in turf battles over IDM. Nevertheless, the smaller the administrative, claims and support staff and the fewer computer systems needed as the result of combining occupational and nonoccupational programs, the greater the administrative savings.[7]

Streamlining the administrative process for filing occupational and nonoccupational claims and using a single claims management system bring another benefit: timely management of an absence. This is critical for influencing employee expectations and bringing about an early and positive closing of the claim.

While these administrative advantages significantly impact a company's indirect costs, they do not account for the large, direct cost savings IDM promises. For those savings, IDM confronts disability costs.

Disability Costs

The primary attractiveness of IDM to most managers is its ability to significantly control disability expenditures leading to reduced disability costs. However, cost control and cost reduction are not the same thing. It is one thing to simply cut costs by reducing access or eliminating benefits and another to control how funds are expended. Controlling costs is the aim of IDM. This means expense is managed so funds are spent effectively, producing the desired outcome. An example is the sports medicine approach to disability medical care. Such an approach pushes for quick medical diagnosis and early, appropriate treatment interventions. The concept is that employees are like professional athletes, who when injured do not take several weeks off and see if things get better. On the contrary, they immediately seek the cause and extent of the injury and receive aggressive treatments that allow them to return to the field as quickly as possible. It is an approach that has been proven cost effective for businesses as well.[8]

In calculating disability cost savings it is important to first understand the total cost of disability. Total disability costs are the sum of direct and indirect (also referred to as hidden) costs.[9] While there is some disagreement as to which costs belong in which category, there is no doubt that for all but the most diligent companies total disability costs are greater than what is routinely measured. Exhibit 5A lists items generally included in the total cost of disability by category.

TOTAL DISABILITY COSTS

Direct Costs	Indirect Costs
Medical payments	Lost productivity
Lost-time wages	Overtime
Administrative costs	Temporary hires
Disability management	Training
Insurance costs	Customer satisfaction
Litigation expenses	Employee morale

National surveys of employers[10] suggest total disability costs equal between 4% and 16% of total payroll costs. This wide range reflects differences between types of business (industry), company size, state, number of work locations and richness of benefit plans. A benchmark frequently used for large company comparisons is 8% of payroll.[11] At this level of expense, direct costs make up 4.5% of total costs, indirect costs 3% and disability management 1.2% of total dollars spent. A further breakdown shows sick leave and short-term disability (STD) to be 36% of direct costs, with workers' compensation 30%, long-term disability (LTD) 10% and FICA tax 24%, respectively. The largest contributor to indirect costs is sick leave and STD (86%), followed by LTD (8%) and workers' compensation (6%).

A 1998 study of disability costs by Unum,[12] a large national disability insurer, reported that direct disability costs make up 52% of the total cost of disability and average $2,860 per employee each year. Indirect costs average 35% or $971 per employee and disability management costs (defined as claims management, employee assistance programs, safety and wellness, and return-to-work programs) run 13% of total disability costs and $352 per employee. These numbers are a significant expense by any measure.

Another study of the total cost of disability[13] found the distribution of costs shown in Exhibit 5B.

It is clear from the above studies there is no consensus on the total cost of disability. This points to the need for a company to investigate its own expenditures. To calculate its true disability costs, however, a company must obtain accurate data.

Exhibit 5B

BREAKDOWN OF TOTAL DISABILITY COSTS

Disability Costs as a Percent of Payroll

Lost Production	2.94%
Workers' Comp Pay	1.06
FICA	1.02
Workers' Comp Medical	.78
STD/LTD Medical	.51
LTD Pay	.32
Nonmedical Disability Benefits	.32

A basic principle of management is "what can be measured can be managed and what can be managed can be improved." Understanding what and where the costs are is a prerequisite for both controlling costs and reducing them. The inability to measure the true cost of disability alone argues for the adoption of IDM. The hallmarks of IDM are the singular claims management process and the single information system that not only gathers comprehensive disability data, but also makes it available in near real time for decision making and analysis.

"Tell me how much I will save with IDM" is a frequent query some executives make when they are resisting the move to IDM. The irony of such a request is they know it is nearly impossible to predict savings when current costs are unknown. Further, the main concern is usually focused on direct costs when reduced expenditures are just part of the disability management process savings. It can be argued that the improved productivity, enhanced employee satisfaction and improved customer relations that come with returning employees to work sooner are more critical to profitability and long-term business success than are short-term dollar savings. The above notwithstanding, the cost savings reported by companies that have implemented IDM are impressive.

- ◆ Cable Systems International, a 2,000 employee copper cable manufacturer, reported a total disability cost savings of 86% in 1996 over previous year expense following the implementation of an IDM program.[14]

◆ Champion International, a major producer of paper products with 18,000 employees, began to move to IDM in 1992 (and expects a fully integrated program in 1999). They revealed a savings trend from 1992 to 1996 that took workers' compensation from $24 million a year to $13½ million (44%), and STD and LTD costs down 8%.[15]

◆ Owens Corning, PacBell, Steelcase, General Electric and a host of others have also reported impressive savings following the implementation of IDM programs.

In its 1998 report on disability, The Washington Business Group on Health (WBGH), a nonprofit health care interest group, reported the average total disability cost saving for companies using IDM was 16%.[16] When fully in place and properly executed, IDM can deliver additional savings until cost reduction reaches a point of diminishing returns.

Disability Data

Both human resource and risk managers need accurate and complete data regarding disability claims. One of the significant drawbacks to separate information systems for the management of occupational and nonoccupational disability is that information critical for decision making is not centralized and often unavailable.

In most companies, information regarding workers' compensation cases is readily available because workers' compensation is driven by state statutes that mandate defined reporting requirements. Companies must collect basic information, organize it by state and business location and report it to state regulatory agencies.[17] Failure to do so subjects the company to fines and potential litigation. Although workers' compensation reporting requirements differ by state, generally data on the number and types of injuries/illnesses incurred, medical costs and lost-time costs must be reported. This basic information is usually adequate to review where injuries/incidents occur in the workplace and where money is spent. It does not, however, provide detailed information on medical utilization, return to work and other manageable activities. Further, if companies have salary continuation programs and/or other supplemental pay benefits, this data is not captured in the normal workers' compensation reporting metrics.

Comprehensive nonoccupational disability information is even more difficult to obtain. Most companies do not have a sound plan or method for capturing nonoccupational lost-time data (cause, duration, etc.), let alone other related costs. Fewer still have the ability to tie in associated group medical cost information.

Until the mid- to late-1980s, nonoccupational medical costs were considered a cost of doing business, and there was a reluctance to manage them or any related absences. Today, however, business reality has changed. An absence from work is an absence from work, and it makes little difference if the reason is occupational or not. With any unplanned absence, work is not getting done, and there are a host of employee and business costs that a company must bear. Progressive businesses do not dwell on the cause of a specific absence, but instead emphasize the management of all nonscheduled absences and the control of their associated costs. This is usually based on timely medical care and a speedy return to work. The underpinning of this effort is information. If companies are to be effective in managing medically related absence and controlling costs, they must have access to accurate information on a timely basis. Any sound IDM program will meet those fundamental management needs.

Compounding the data availability issue are the multiple information systems most companies use to capture absence and medical data. Many of these systems typically fall under the responsibility of several different departments, organizations, providers or vendors, and may not be compatible. This lack of a uniform and centralized information system is a major hindrance in obtaining the data important for program analysis and evaluation. It also hinders case management and the development of targeted prevention programs.

The implementation of an IDM program has a significant impact on these accessibility issues. A central component of any true IDM program is a single information system for both occupational and nonoccupational claims. With the most progressive IDM claims systems this permits collection of information starting at initial claim notification. With common claim intake and case management, data for both occupational and nonoccupational claims resides in one system and in one comprehensive file. Adjusters and managers have access to all relevant claim-related information: demographic, event/incident, personnel, medical, pay and claims history. Information can be viewed or collated by subject and downloaded for analysis. The availability of comprehensive data is a process improvement over multiple information systems and offers timely decision support for managers.

Is the Company Ready for IDM?

Once a company understands the components and potential benefits of IDM, the next step should be to evaluate the current situation. Before taking the leap to integrate, there should be a recognition of the areas where IDM will provide the biggest savings and greatest management advantages. The company must also set goals to be achieved through integration. Experience to date has shown that not all employers pursue integration for the same reasons. While lowering medical costs and associated lost time are implicit motivation, improved quality of service; increased employee satisfaction, recruitment and retention; and the desire to be "the best in class" have all been cited as reasons to pursue IDM.

The crafting of reasonable expectations cannot be done without a clear assessment of current benefit plans, processes and costs and an honest appraisal of the company's appetite for change. Identification of potential obstacles and barriers to change within the organization is a critical success factor for IDM.

Appendix 5A on page 72 provides a checklist that can be a helpful tool in assessing a company's readiness for IDM. Once completed, it helps identify the areas and performance issues where benefit plan design, administrative processes, cost and information improvements can be made. Appendix 5B on page 79 is an IDM Readiness Matrix, developed by IntegraComp, that helps an employer pinpoint the facilitators and obstacles within its company and programs.

Another important aspect of conducting a front-end assessment of current disability programs and performance is providing a clear vision to potential vendors. If a company can articulate what it expects to obtain from the implementation of an IDM program, vendors should be able to design a program that meets the company's desired specifications. To have realistic expectations of an IDM program, however, it is important to keep in mind that IDM is not a panacea for all disability problems. A well-designed and executed IDM program can deliver administrative and process improvements, enhance data collection and availability, and reduce total disability costs, but it is not a substitute for carefully designed disability benefit plans and a company culture where employees value work and follow proper behaviors. There is more money to be saved from properly designed and coordinated disability plans than there is from managing events after they have taken place.

The disability assessment process is best conducted by a dedicated team. A company officer should lead this team. Failure to have senior leadership manage the assessment effort subjects it to internal political pressure, the inability to access information and uncooperative individuals and organizations. The team should also include a cross section of managers and staff from the various organizations that have direct responsibility for executing and/or supporting the company's disability program. Knowledgeable individuals from audit, claims management, benefits, finance, human resources, information technology, medical, risk management, safety and workers' compensation can assist in objectively documenting the administrative, cost and information characteristics of the current disability benefits program. It may be helpful as well to have an outside consultant or facilitator to help guide and plan the assessment process and interpret results. In addition, representatives from providers and vendors that support the current programs can also be helpful team members, especially if they hold critical information. The complexity of the company's programs and the difficulty of acquiring information necessary to evaluate current programs fully should drive team size and make-up.

A recommended list of assessment team members and their roles follows.

- ◆ **Team Leader:** A senior executive (at the officer level with decision-making authority) who reports to the COO, CEO or president. The team leader supplies in-depth knowledge of the business and a clear understanding of the project mission. Ideally this person will bridge existing gaps between human resources and risk management.

- ◆ **Consultant:** An outside expert, the IDM consultant knows benefit plans and costs, risk control, data analysis and organizational management.

- ◆ **Financial Lead:** A finance manager, with knowledge of budgeting, cost accounting, financial analysis and business planning, serves as the financial lead.

- ◆ **Human Resources Lead:** A senior human resources manager supplies detailed information on personnel policies, benefit plans and strategy.

- ◆ **Information Technology (IT) Lead:** An individual with knowledge of the company's computer systems and programs, the information technology lead advises on and assists in the retrieval and manipulation of data.

- ◆ **Medical Lead:** The medical lead is a health care professional with knowledge of company disability policies and procedures. Capable of evaluating medical care programs, treatments, outcomes, disability management procedures, physical capacity assessments and return-to-work programs, this person is the liaison to provider networks and outside medical professionals.

- ◆ **Supervisor:** An operational manager provides the team with the perspective of one who must deal with the day-to-day business consequences of disability and the efficacy of administrative procedures.

- **Risk Management Lead:** A manager level individual, with a knowledge of risk operations, policies and insurance, serves as the risk management lead.
- **Safety Lead:** The safety lead is a manager with in-depth knowledge of the company's safety strategy and plans and knowledgeable in return-to-work and modified work programs. This person also benefits the team by having a good working relationship with operational managers.
- **Staff Support:** Clerical and support staff collate data and provide office support to the assessment team.

A key ingredient of any assessment team is leadership. The leader should be a strong consensus builder, capable of inspiring diversely knowledgeable individuals to act as a team. It is the leader's responsibility to ensure that the team defines its mission, determines the assessment plan, divides responsibilities and sets time lines. It is also the leader's responsibility to promote communication within the team and throughout the organization whenever appropriate.

The end result of the assessment effort should be an objective evaluation of all aspects of the company's disability management programs (especially what is working and what requires adjustment) in light of the company's business objectives. Following the assessment, which should be documented, the findings can be reviewed in contrast to the advantages of an IDM program. This provides an indication of the areas in which IDM will provide the most benefit. Once this is established, the formal planning process for the design and implementation of an IDM program that meets the company's specific needs can begin.

Summary

Integrated disability management is a progressive management practice that combines the management and administrative processes of occupational and nonoccupational disability benefits into a single system. IDM permits companies to manage disability and control related costs. It also has a positive impact on employee satisfaction and customer relationships.

IDM programs have five components:
1. A single claims intake and notification process
2. A single claims management system
3. A common medical case management process
4. A common return-to-work program
5. A single database.

It is the synergy of unifying these processes under single management and the accessibility of comprehensive claim and disability information that make IDM powerful. Successful IDM programs are characterized by improved benefit processes, ease of access to information and the reduction of total disability costs.

The case for adopting an IDM program is sound. Companies considering such a move should begin by assessing the current state of their disability benefit programs in three basic areas: administrative processes, costs and information availability. Another consideration to be reviewed is employee satisfaction with the current disability benefit program. Companies should appoint a multidisciplinary team to conduct an objective evaluation of their programs. The completed assessment of "what is" will form the basis for process improvement and allow management to determine whether and where an IDM program will be most advantageous.

Endnotes

1. T. Corcoran and T. E. Klett, "Managing Disability Past, Present and Future," *Benefits Quarterly,* Fourth Quarter 1997.

2. "Disability Incidence Higher for Downsizing Firms, Costs Rise, But Integrating Effort Lowers Costs Studies Show," *Spencer's Research Reports on Employee Benefits,* 29 August, 1997.

3. An analysis of the American businesses by Sedgwick CMS in 1998 found that no Fortune 500 company implemented an IDM program in 1997 and fewer than 100 companies across the country had IDM programs in place in 1998.

4. D. A. North and K. Higdon, "Landmark Survey: Best Practices in Integrated Disability Management," *Journal of Workers' Compensation,* Winter 1998.

5. C. Cather, "How Brokers View Integrated Benefits" (presentation at the annual meeting of the Integrated Benefits Institute, March 1997).

6. There are legal issues to consider when advocating and implementing an integrated information system. Please refer to "Privacy Concerns," in Chapter Four.

7. It is important, however, that IDM units be staffed at a level driven by workload (claim count) and the ability to do the job (skill). Simply cutting staff by increasing the number (or type) of claims an adjuster must handle to effect a savings negates the benefit of using an IDM program. It also reduces quality and service. The appropriate staff size is an issue that should be addressed during the planning phase of IDM implementation.

8. The Integrated Benefits Institute investigated the sports medicine concept in workers' compensation. The results revealed that in cases where there was an aggressive push for diagnosis and early intervention, companies spend more money early in the disability case on medical intervention and treatment. This aggressiveness resulted in faster returns to work (shorter absence). The study suggests that a sports medicine approach has the potential to reduce total dollars spent per case as a result of shorter durations of absence and lower wage replacement costs.

9. Unum Life Insurance Company of America, *Insight* 3, no. 2 (1996).

10. Corcoran and Klett, *Managing Disability;* Watson Wyatt Worldwide and the Washington Business Group on Health, *Staying at Work: Improving Productivity Through Integrated Disability Management* (1998).

11. Unum Life Insurance Company of America, *Disability Matters: A Report on Managing Disability Costs* (1998).

12. Ibid.

13. IntegraComp LLC (Deerfield, IL), unpublished research, 1996.

14. B. Caldwell, "Employers Report Reduced Cost Due to Workers' Compensation Initiatives," *Employee Benefit Review,* March 1998.

15. "Champion International Corporation," *Integrated Benefits Institute Review,* September 1997.

16. Watson Wyatt, *Staying at Work.*

17. *Workers Comp: Volume I* (International Risk Management Institute, Inc., 1995).

Appendix 5A
IDM ASSESSMENT CHECKLIST

The purpose of this checklist is to provide a framework for assessing company disability programs in three basic areas: process, costs and information. This checklist is not all-inclusive, and evaluators should conduct assessments in other areas of interest specific to their organization. Following the formal assessment, costs and operational information should be benchmarked to past performance, national and industry data. A contrast can then be made between current programs and the advantages provided by an IDM program.

I.   Plan, Program and Process Information

    A. Demographics

         1. What is the company's population?   FTE: PTE:

         2. What is the company's total payroll? _____

         3. How many separate locations (plants, offices, etc.) does the company have? _____

    B. Benefit Plans Listing: What disability and health care benefits does the company offer? Circle all that apply.

1. Short-term disability (STD)	Yes	No
2. Long-term disability (LTD)	Yes	No
3. Sick leave/Salary continuation	Yes	No
4. Personal time off (PTO)	Yes	No
5. Group health plans	Yes	No

If yes, what types? (Circle all that apply.)

Indemnity   HMO   PPO   POS   Other

6. How many different providers does the company use?		
7. Vision care	Yes	No
8. Dental care	Yes	No
9. Employee assistance program (EAP)	Yes	No
10. Health care savings account	Yes	No
11. Dependent care savings account	Yes	No
12. Other plan information _____		

C. Disability Plans Description: Describe below the characteristics of the listed disability benefits.
  1. STD plan
     a. Eligibility requirements and employee contributions: _____
     b. Pay benefits
        i. Off-sets
        ii. Elimination period
     c. Length of plan
     d. Notification requirements
  2. LTD plan
     a. Eligibility requirements and employee contributions: _____
     b. Pay benefits
        i. Off-sets
        ii. Elimination period
     c. Length of plan
     d. Notification requirements

D. Insurance and Related Vendors
  1. Are you insured for the following coverages?
     a. WC?   Yes   No
     b. STD?   Yes   No
     c. LTD?   Yes   No
  2. Are you self-insured/self-funded for the following coverages?
     a. WC?   Yes   No
     b. STD?   Yes   No
     c. LTD?   Yes   No
  3. Are you self-administered for the following coverages?
     a. WC?   Yes   No
     b. STD?   Yes   No
     c. LTD?   Yes   No
  4. If not self-administered, who is your TPA?
     a. WC?
     b. STD?
     c. LTD?
  5. List the types of claims they manage: _____
  6. If you are insured for WC and/or offer disability or health insurance, list the types of coverages you have and the insurer.
     a. WC, insurance carrier:
     b. STD, insurance carrier:
     c. LTD, insurance carrier:
     d. Group health, insurance carrier:
     e. Other insurance, type and insurance carrier:
  7. Do you use a broker?   Yes   No

8. List all brokers: _____

9. Do you use a benefits consultant?   Yes   No

10. List all consultants: _____

11. What organization in the company is responsible for
    a. Workers' compensation (WC)?
    b. STD?
    c. LTD?

E. Administrative Processes

1. Does a single organization manage all disability cases? Yes   No

2. If not, what organizations manage disability cases? _____

3. Is there a single claims notification procedure?   Yes   No

4. If not, what organizations do claims intake? _____

5. Circle all methods of claims intake that apply.

    1-800   Walk-up   Electronic Intranet

    Electronic Internet   Other: _____

6. Are First Reports of Injury filed electronically?   Yes   No

7. Is FMLA tracked for every medically related
    absence meeting FMLA requirements?   Yes   No

8. Is the process for populating the claims management
    system automatic from the claims intake system?   Yes   No

9. Are the intake and claims management system linked? Yes   No

10. How are supervisor and managers notified
    of a disability claim? _____

11. Who manages the return-to-work process? _____

12. Is there a common claims handling process across
    benefits (occ/non-occ)?   Yes   No

13. Are all disability claims handled by one organization? Yes   No

14. Do nurses conduct medical management and interact
    with providers when appropriate?   Yes   No

15. Is one set of treatment protocols used for both
    occupational and nonoccupational cases?   Yes   No

16. Is a single provider network used for all disability? Yes   No

17. Are claims handled from a central location?   Yes   No

18. Are occupational and nonoccupational claims
    information contained in one database and accessible
    to adjusters to avoid unnecessary duplications
    and investigations?   Yes   No

19. If WC liability is unclear, are nonoccupational benefits
    paid if available until a determination is made?   Yes   No

20. Does the company have a RTW program
    (both occupational and nonoccupational)?   Yes   No

21. Is there a single return-to-work (RTW) process
    for all disability?   Yes   No

22. Does a nurse handle RTW coordination?   Yes   No

23. If not, who does? _____

24. Is there a central point of contact for light duty
    jobs at each company location?   Yes   No

25. Is there a central appeals contact for WC
    and disability claims?   Yes   No

26. Is there a central point of contact for all claims?   Yes   No

II.   Disability Costs

A.   What is the total number of workers' compensation cases
     for [specify time period]? _____

B.   What is the total cost of WC (wages + medical + administration) for
     [specify time period]? _____

C.   How many WC cases were medical only for
     [specify time period]? _____

D.   How much of the WC expense is medical only for
     [specify time period]? _____

E.   How many WC cases were lost-time cases for
     [specify time period]? _____

F.   How much of the WC expense is lost-time wages for
     [specify time period]? _____

G.   What is the total number of STD cases for
     [specify time period]? _____

H.   What is the ratio of WC cases to STD cases for
     [specify time period]? _____

I.   What is the cost of STD benefits for
     [specify time period]? _____

J.   Are medical costs associated with STD tracked?   Yes   No

K.   If so, how much was spent on medical care related
     to STD cases for [specify time period]? _____

L.   What is the total cost of STD (benefits + medical +
     administration) for [specify time period]? _____

M. What is the total number of LTD cases for
   [specify time period]? _____

N. What is the cost of LTD benefits for
   [specify time period]? _____

O. Are medical costs associated with LTD tracked?   Yes   No

P. If so, how much was spent on medical care related
   to LTD cases for [specify time period]? _____

Q. What is the total cost of LTD (benefits + medical +
   administration) for [specify time period]? _____

R. What is the ratio of STD cases to LTD cases for
   [specify time period]? _____

S. Calculate the following component costs of disability for
   [specify time period]:
   1. WC as a percent of payroll _____
   2. WC costs per employee _____
   3. WC medical as a percent of payroll _____
   4. WC cost per medical-only case _____
   5. WC lost time indemnity payments as a
      percent of payroll _____
   6. STD as a percent of payroll _____
   7. STD costs per employee _____
   8. STD medical costs as a percent of STD _____
   9. STD medical costs per case _____
   10. STD medical cost as a percent of payroll _____
   11. LTD as a percent of payroll _____
   12. LTD costs per employee _____
   13. LTD medical costs as a percent of LTD _____
   14. LTD medical costs per case _____
   15. LTD medical costs as a percent of payroll _____

T. What are the total **direct costs** of disability in the
   following categories for [specify time period]?
   1. Medical payments
      a. WC _____
      b. Group health (related to STD, LTD and other) _____
   2. Lost-time benefits
      a. WC _____
      b. STD _____
      c. LTD _____

3. Administrative costs
   a. WC _____
   b. STD _____
   c. LTD _____
   d. Group health _____
   e. Other disability-related benefits _____

4. Disability management costs
   a. WC _____
   b. STD _____
   c. LTD _____
   d. Other disability-related benefits _____

5. Insurance costs
   a. WC _____
   b. STD _____
   c. LTD _____
   d. Group health _____

6. Litigation expense
   a. WC _____
   b. Other (specify) _____

U. What are the total **indirect costs** of disability in the following categories?

   1. Lost production _____

   2. Disability-related overtime _____

   3. Cost of temp hires _____

   4. Training/retraining expense _____

V. What are the costs associated with the following?

   1. Customer satisfaction (lost/unhappy customers) _____

   2. Employee morale _____

W. Are the indirect/hidden costs of disability routinely
    included in the company's calculation of its
    total cost of disability?   Yes   No

X. Calculate the following:

   1. Total cost of disability _____

   2. Disability as a percent of total payroll _____

   3. Disability as a cost per employee _____

   4. Direct costs as a percent of total disability costs _____

   5. Indirect costs as a percent of total disability costs _____

   6. Administration costs as a percent of total disability costs _____

III. Data/Information Availability

A.	Are disability records and data computerized?	Yes	No
B.	Are both WC and nonoccupational disability claims maintained on a common database?	Yes	No
C.	If not, are the different databases/systems compatible?	Yes	No
D.	Does the HR database interface with the claims management database?	Yes	No
E.	Is a single agency responsible for the claims and disability database?	Yes	No
F.	Is a medical management module a component of the claims management information system?	Yes	No
G.	Is medical case management information data included in the electronic claims file?	Yes	No
H.	Do you have on-line access to WC data?	Yes	No
I.	Do you have on-line access to STD data?	Yes	No
J.	Do you have on-line access to LTD data?	Yes	No
K.	Are regular disability reports provided to managers?	Yes	No
L.	Do reports include frequency, category and cost information?	Yes	No
M.	List routine reports: _____		
N.	Can customized reports for WC and nonoccupational claims be produced on demand?	Yes	No
O.	Is the information management system Windows based?	Yes	No

Appendix 5B
IDM READINESS MATRIX

KEY ELEMENT	FACILITATORS	OBSTACLES	NEUTRAL[1]
Culture			
Approach to business	Entrepreneurial	Risk adverse	
Attitude toward employees	Empowering	Overly paternalistic	
Profitability	Low profit margins	Unprofitable	High profit margins
Return to work	◆ Common modified duty program for occupational and nonoccupational injuries ◆ Strong RTW philosophy ◆ Strong work ethic	No RTW program	Formal RTW program for occupational injuries only
Safety	Best in class safety program	No or very limited safety program	Basic OSHA compliance safety program

Appendix 5B (continued)
IDM READINESS MATRIX

KEY ELEMENT	FACILITATORS	OBSTACLES	NEUTRAL[1]
Organizational Structure	Centralized	Decentralized	
Current Environment	Stable	Labor issues	Company-wide re-engineering or re-engineering of benefits only
Management Support	Upper management is sponsor	◆ Sponsor not decision maker ◆ Low priority for upper management	

Integrated Disability Management—An Employer's Guide

Appendix 5B (continued)
IDM READINESS MATRIX

KEY ELEMENT	FACILITATORS	OBSTACLES	NEUTRAL[1]
Benefits			
Design	◆ Minimal variance in benefits among different locations, employee class ◆ Good medical management procedures in place, WC, STD, LTD ◆ Employer choice state(s) for WC medical care ◆ Some elements of integration in place (e.g., common notification procedure, integrated LTD and STD, single provider network for all disabilities)	◆ Generous benefits provide disabled employee with 100%+ net pay ◆ Employee choice state(s) for WC medical care	Good medical management procedure in workers' compensation
Administration	WC and nonoccupational benefits administered through same department and management	WC and nonoccupational benefits administered through different traditionally noninteractive departments (turf issues)	

Appendix 5B (continued)
IDM READINESS MATRIX

KEY ELEMENT	FACILITATORS	OBSTACLES	NEUTRAL[1]
Labor			
Support	Supportive	Resistant	Specific benefit plans governed by union contracts

Demographics			◆ Predominantly
			  –Older or younger
			  –Female or male
			  –Urban or rural
			  –Blue or white collar
			◆ High or low turnover rates
			◆ Area high or low unemployment

Appendix 5B (continued)
IDM READINESS MATRIX

KEY ELEMENT	FACILITATORS	OBSTACLES	NEUTRAL[1]
Technology	◆ Resources to integrate systems ◆ Systems developed inhouse ◆ State-of-the-art systems	◆ Multiple systems ◆ Multiple platforms ◆ Purchased systems ◆ Antiquated systems	Resources to integrate data (at a minimum)
Vendors/Resources			
Availability	Current vendors have capability to integrate	Limited vendor choices	
Experience	Potential vendors experienced in integration	Potential vendors have limited to no experience	
Quality	Potential vendors provide best practice services	Potential vendors not recognized for quality	
Flexibility	Potential vendors able to design program around company's needs	Potential vendors have limited to no capacity to customize	

Appendix 5B (continued)
IDM READINESS MATRIX

KEY ELEMENT	FACILITATORS	OBSTACLES	NEUTRAL[1]
Measurement Information	Total (direct and indirect) cost of disability known	Data not systematically collected to date and specific numbers not known	
Need	Opportunities for dollars savings	Limited opportunity for dollars savings	

1. Neither facilitator nor obstacle to readiness but may impact design, rate of change or roll-out success.

Source: IntegraComp.

A Consultant Partner

Movement from a series of freestanding, disconnected programs to a single integrated service for disability management has far-reaching implications within a company. Many employers find it advantageous to retain a consultant to help them navigate what may be, at times, shark-infested waters! The need for or advisability of seeking assistance is not necessarily dictated by the size of the company but rather by the availability or absence of internal resources that can be applied to achieve stated goals within the desired time frame. Consultants possess neither universal answers nor infinite wisdom, but they should possess the skills and experience to help the client (employer) articulate a vision, solve problems and achieve defined goals.

While employers may be shocked by what they perceive as exorbitant fees—particularly if they are not in the habit of using consulting services—they will usually find it is more cost effective to use a consultant than to redeploy or hire additional internal resources. Before the decision to hire a consultant is made, it is important for the in-house sponsors of IDM to consider what role the consultant will play and what specific tasks will be assigned. As always, management of expectations is critical, and the selection of the right consultant will depend upon the clear definition of role and tasks.

Chapter 6

Selecting the Right Partners

by Janet R. Douglas

Role of the Consultant

Ideally the consultant will be involved from the time the employer begins to consider IDM. The role of the consultant is to act as business advisor, facilitator and problem solver for the client. Specific tasks include working with a company task force to develop a philosophy, vision and action plan for IDM; helping the company determine its readiness for IDM, its program design and vendor selection; and aiding the development of benchmarks and measurements, audits and evaluations, to quantify the success of IDM. A consultant can also be invaluable in employee communication and change management. Since IDM calls for individuals and departments that, historically, have had little or no contact with each other, to work closely and cooperatively, it can be helpful to have an objective, knowledgeable outsider to help forge relationships and build a team. Whether the impetus for IDM is coming from upper or middle management, the consultant can be an effective messenger between the various constituencies.

How to Find a Consultant

Many large companies already have relationships with consulting firms. An existing relationship is often an excellent place to start. A trusted business advisor may also know an appropriate resource either inside or outside his own company. Beware, however, the "instant expert." Consulting firms have been known to grow expertise overnight in response to a client's request, so it is important to show due diligence regardless of the source of referral.

If there are no existing relationships with consulting firms or, for whatever reason, a decision is made to look elsewhere, there are several other reliable sources of information on consultants. Trade and professional journals generally contain articles on IDM written by consultant practitioners, and the names of people who are active in IDM show up frequently on educational programs and national seminars and conferences. Networking through human resource and risk management professional organizations will also yield reliable information and referrals. Employers should not hesitate to call their peers in companies that have already tackled IDM to find out with whom they have worked and what the outcomes have been.

Hallmarks of a Good Consultant

Much like lawyers, consultants often find themselves the butt of jokes, such as "the person who steals a client's watch and then charges him big bucks to tell him the time," or the recipient of criticism for charging high fees and failing to add value. Unlike the law, however, consulting is not a regulated profession. There are no licenses, no qualifying examinations and no national standards. Much of the criticism aimed at consultants may be richly deserved in an environment where the only requirement to become a consultant is the ability to get someone to pay for the service. Needless to say, there are many qualified and ethical consultants who provide valuable service, but the message to employers is clear: *Caveat emptor!*

How then does the employer recognize and choose a good consultant? There are criteria by which an individual consultant or a consulting firm as a whole can be ranked. These include:

- ◆ Integrity
- ◆ Background, education and training
- ◆ Experience
- ◆ Content expertise
- ◆ Interpersonal skills
- ◆ Reputation.

To determine how well a consultant meets these criteria, an employer should interview the consultant, obtain references and see samples of the work product. The employer should seek answers to the following questions:

- ◆ *Does the consultant exhibit integrity?*
    - –Does the consultant answer questions openly and honestly?
    - –Does the consultant share confidential details of other consulting engagements? (Count on it–if someone else's secrets aren't safe, no one's are!)
    - –Do samples of work products seem remarkably similar? (Does it appear that clients receive "off-the-shelf" work products for consultant fees? Or does the consultant sell new clients duplicates of a product created for and purchased by another client?)
    - –Does another client's name show up in proposals or reports sent out as examples of the consultant's work product?
    - –Is the consultant willing to sign a nondisclosure agreement?
    - –Is the consultant critical of others in his firm, of other clients?
- ◆ *Are the consultant's background, education and training appropriate for this project? Are they impressive?*
    - –Does the consultant's background show concentration in areas relevant to IDM? (In nursing or other clinical professions? Disability management? Human resources? Workers' compensation or disability claims management?)
    - –Does the consultant's resume list recent continuing education in a relevant field?

♦ *Is the consultant's experience relevant to the role and tasks required of him?*
  – Has the consultant worked on projects similar to this one?
  – Has the consultant worked with similar companies?
  – What hands-on experience with health, disability or workers' compensation does the consultant have?
  – Can the consultant provide references for similar work?
♦ *What is the level of the consultant's expertise in IDM?*
  – Has the consultant published or presented material at seminars on the subject of IDM?
  – Does the consultant have an advanced degree or professional designation relevant to IDM?
  – Can the consultant answer in-depth questions and identify appropriate resources for IDM?
♦ *Does the consultant possess good interpersonal and communication skills?*
  – Does the consultant listen?
  – Does the consultant make eye contact?
  – Does the consultant establish good rapport?
  – Is the consultant's appearance well-groomed and professional?
  – Does the consultant speak well? (Beware of *ums, ahs,* and *y'knows,* slang, buzzwords and offensive language! Look for someone who explains clearly, without condescension.)
  – Is the consultant's demeanor friendly yet professional? (No one has time to follow after a consultant and smooth ruffled feathers!)
♦ *What is the consultant's reputation?*
  – Is the consultant well-known in the field of IDM? (Watch out for too much hype.)
  – Has the consultant published and presented? Is this work respected?
  – Does the consultant have a positive reputation among professional peers?
  – How highly do other clients rank the consultant?

Consultant Fees

A significant part of the management of expectations in consulting engagements relates to fees. Often when the client is disappointed in the result of a consulting engagement and questions its value, it is because certain vital information was never communicated. A common complaint from employers is, "For what I paid, I thought I'd get a lot more." The consultant counters, "They bought and paid for a basic Ford, but they expected a fully-loaded Cadillac."

Consultants usually price their proposal on the basis of time multiplied by hourly rate, plus the cost of out-of-pocket expenses. Most consulting firms require that individual consultants generate at least three times their annual salary in client fees. Hourly rates are nothing more than an internal cost-accounting system for the consultant.

The pricing of a consulting engagement is an imprecise art at best. *Parkinson's Law,* which, stated simply, means that if you have all day to write a postcard it takes all day to write it, applies to consulting engagements in triplicate! Ideally, the client and the consultant work closely together to first agree on the goal, then to scope out the parameters of the engagement. The consultant can then give an estimate of how much time it will take to complete the assigned tasks. The number of hours are multiplied by hourly rates (determined by skill levels and experience) and a project budget is determined.

Problems occur when the client sets expectations that cannot be met for the amount of money approved in the consulting budget, or the consultant seriously underestimates the amount of time it will take to complete the required actions. Regular, effective communication will do much to alleviate potential problems.

To get the best possible outcomes the client (employer) must determine that consulting funds are available in sufficient amounts to buy the services required. The consultant can then "cut the coat according to the cloth" and ensure that client expectations will be met. Consultants should commit to a not-to-exceed amount for an engagement and, if requested, submit to penalties for late or subquality work product.

A Final Word About Consultant Choice

Finally, when all discussion and due diligence have taken place, the most important issue to consider in selecting a consultant or team of consultants is fit. Does this individual or team fit with the organization? Is there good chemistry? Do members of the task force want to work side-by-side with the consultant or team through difficult and trying situations? Is there a level of trust and simpatico that indicates on a visceral level that this would be the right choice? Are the people who dealt with the task force during the negotiation phase the ones who will show up when the engagement begins?

Remember, in consulting bigger is not always better. What counts is having a consultant who is knowledgeable, creative and low-maintenance, who delivers high-quality service on time and on budget.

A Service Provider Partner for Claims Administration and Disability Management

For the employer, the selection of a service provider partner is a critically important step. Preliminary work will dictate whether an insurance carrier or third-party administrator is required. Whether working with or without the assistance of a consultant partner, it is vital to conduct adequate due diligence and to be sure the selected service provider can truly execute the employer's vision of IDM.

Principles of the Selection Process

The principles involved in the selection process are fundamentally similar to those involved in picking a consultant partner. There are four things to consider in the initial approach to selection: ability, experience, cost and fit.

◆ **Ability:** Can the service provider meet the needs (technical, professional, ideological and geographical) that the employer has identified?

◆ **Experience:** Does the service provider have a proven track record in implementation of IDM? What is the profile of the companies it is currently serving? Is there a match? If the service provider does not have experience (and, in an emerging field such as IDM someone has to be the first client), does it have clear top-down support within its organization for new initiatives? Also, would it be willing to reflect the lack of experience in cost, at least for the first year? It is not always bad to be the first client if there is a real partnership and a strong sense of learning together.

◆ **Cost:** This is an area where an employer again needs to follow the buyer beware rule. There are many, many ways of pricing services. In comparing responses to requests for proposal, it is vital for the employer to understand what the various prices include and, more importantly, do not include. What appears to be the cheapest program may yield the lowest return on investment for the employer. The most expensive program may, in the final analysis, be the most cost effective. Perhaps the most important feature to concentrate on is not cost but value.

An appropriate pricing structure for an IDM program will include the impact of the program on the total cost of disability. If the impact cannot be measured, then the success of the program will be forever in question. The employer will question the value of a program that cannot be quantified and will deem it "not worth the money." If, on the other hand, the proposed program includes a model for impact assessment, the potential for success and perceived "high value for the money" is greatly enhanced.

◆ **Fit:** The last, but certainly not the least, issue is fit. Is there a strong sense among the stakeholders at the company that they can partner effectively with a particular service provider? It is a good sign if they have worked together in the past and enjoyed a positive relationship. If, in contrast, their prior shared history has not been good, the chances of a successful outcome may be diminished. Will the individuals involved in the selection process be members of the account team or will they disappear into obscurity the moment the contract is signed? It is advisable for the employer to request that the individual(s) who will manage the account be identified and approved prior to completion of negotiation. Obviously, a new, large client will require most service providers to staff up, but the employer certainly has the right to expect that those in leadership roles are seasoned senior employees with enough experience in the service provider's environment to successfully implement the program.

If, as the selection proceeds, there are serious issues about fit for a particular provider, it is generally advisable to heed the warning and move on.

Management

Frequently, when the relationship between an employer and service provider falters, the genesis of the problem can be traced to failure to set and manage expectations on both sides. When selecting a service provider for IDM, it is vital that the employer set forth a clear set of expectations for the service provider and vice versa. The employer must articulate what service is expected. Where, when and how that service will be delivered must be articulated by the service provider. Both employer and service provider will be best served if they can agree upon and adopt a set of best practices that addresses all aspects of the service. A sample set of best practices can be found in Appendices 6A-6C.

Appendix 6A

SAMPLE REQUEST FOR PROPOSAL

EMPLOYER A

REQUEST FOR PROPOSAL
FOR CLAIMS ADMINISTRATION AND
INTEGRATED DISABILITY MANAGEMENT

TABLE OF CONTENTS

PART I: GENERAL INFORMATION AND PROPOSAL SPECIFICATIONS

Employer A Background Information

Employer A will provide the following:

♦ Information on the company's history, nature of business, growth, location(s) and financial status

♦ A detailed description of current programs for managing short- and long-term disability and workers' compensation

♦ A statement of expectation of IDM and the preferred model.

Service Provider Background Information

The service provider will submit information on company history, size, geographic distribution of offices and experience with IDM.

Proposal Specifications

The approach to IDM must include integration of intake, medical management, return to work and information systems. Additionally, the following criteria must be met:

♦ Contract negotiations may be undertaken with the contractors whose proposals and prices and other factors demonstrate their qualifications, responsiveness and capability to perform the services requested. The contract will be developed and written with language that is consistent with limited risk exposure for *Employer A*. Pricing and other factors will be included in the contract.

♦ Rates cannot be changed except on the contract renewal date. Written notice must be given to *Employer A* at least 90 days prior to a contemplated rate change and/or contract renewal. All increases in rates above an adjustment for inflation must be justified, and they must demonstrate necessity. Responders, therefore, are cautioned not to quote fees too far below current market levels.

♦ Service quotes should be provided on an unbundled basis. If discounts are available for combined services, these should be separately noted. Rates should include training materials, management reports, travel, meeting times and any other related expenses. These should be quoted per annum or for the length of the contract.

♦ Each applicant offers and agrees to furnish all items and services upon which the contract is to be negotiated (at the prices offered). Each applicant further agrees to provide its services in compliance with the time frames specified in the contract.

- The TPA will be required to maintain all pertinent records for seven years from the date of activity. All data, including TPA correspondence, is the property of *Employer A* and will be provided, upon request and within reason, in the formats specified by *Employer A*.

- The selected respondent(s) must be financially sound. TPAs must provide annual reports or audited financial reports for the years _____ and _____. The company's most recent _____ quarterly update should also be provided.

- All service quotes must be provided as requested and outlined in Part IV: Financial Format of this RFP. Please follow this format exactly and provide complete information.

- Selection of a TPA will be based on the following criteria:
  –Service capabilities, including specific geographic capabilities, flexibility and responsiveness in dealing with *Employer A's* needs
  –Prior performance record for similar size and type-of-work companies for years _____, _____ and _____
  –Demonstrated ability to assist *Employer A* proactively in meeting its objective of reducing its occupational and nonoccupational disability costs
  –Financial competitiveness
  –Completeness, clarity and accuracy of proposal.
   One or more responders identified by *Employer A* will be invited to make a brief oral presentation and answer questions at a location of *Employer A's* choice. It is anticipated that this presentation will occur during the _____ week of (month), (year). In addition, *Employer A* staff may request an on-site visit to the facility that will be responsible for administering its account.

- It is expected that the selected TPA will carry a $5 million minimum liability insurance policy in *Employer A's* name to cover its errors and omissions.

General Instructions

- **Process:** All questions regarding these specifications should be faxed to _____ (#_____) by (month) (day), (year). A compilation of all vendor questions regarding the RFP and *Employer A's* responses will be sent to all vendors by the end of the day on (month) (day), (year).

  Please submit two copies of your proposal. Proposals must be received on or before 12:00 noon, (month) (day), (year). The copies should be directed to

  > *Person X*
  > *Employer A*
  > *Street Address*
  > *City, State and ZIP Code*

- **Binding commitment:** The written proposal, plus any subsequent offers or representations made during the final evaluation process, will be considered binding commitments by the TPA and will be included in the contract.
- **Time for acceptance:** The TPA agrees to be bound by its proposal for a period of 120 days during which time *Employer A* may request clarification or correction of the proposal for the purpose of evaluation.
- **Time line:** The competitive bidding process involves the following steps and timetable.

Steps	Dates
Specifications to bidders	
Vendor questions regarding RFP	
Proposals due to Employer A	
Analysis of proposals	
Finalists notified	
Finalist interviews	
Site visits (optional)	
Finalists selected	
Contract negotiation	
Implementation date	

Minimum Requirements

- **Internal capabilities:** The selected TPA must demonstrate there is sufficient clerical staff to support consistent, timely workflow by adjusters. Likewise, the TPA must have internal capabilities or contract for an automated data system that can store and analyze *Employer A's* disability data according to established provisions and standards for claims handling and management instructions.

  Do you agree?   ☐ Yes   ☐ No   If no, note exceptions.
- **Release of information:** To be considered for selection, the TPA must be willing to provide copies of medical records, correspondence and other claims management documents to *Employer A* upon request, and must be willing to allow *Employer A* to select and utilize, or reject, additional claims management services (such as rehabilitation, medical cost containment, legal and private investigation) according to criteria

and performance standards that *Employer A* defines. These would be discussed and developed in conjunction with the TPA's knowledge and/or approval.

Do you agree?   □ Yes   □ No   If no, note exceptions.

♦ **Agreement for settlement:** The TPA must agree to confer with *Employer A* prior to making an offer of settlement and must be willing and able to justify the recommendation to settle for the agreed amount. Discretionary settlement levels and the designated staff who perform this service will be developed and included in the contract.

Do you agree?   □ Yes   □ No   If no, note exceptions.

♦ **Development of claims handling instructions:** To be considered, a TPA must be willing to develop claims handling and management instructions with *Employer A* that will be used as a measure of its performance at annual review meetings between the TPA and *Employer A*.

Do you agree?   □ Yes   □ No   If no, note exceptions.

♦ **Right to audit:** *Employer A* reserves the right to audit annually the financial and nonfinancial records of its TPA as these pertain to *Employer A's* IDM program whenever *Employer A* deems it appropriate. Such audits may be performed by *Employer A's* staff or by outside auditors selected by *Employer A*. A 30-day written notice will be provided to the TPA prior to the selected audit date.

Do you agree?   □ Yes   □ No   If no, note exceptions.

♦ **Contract term:** The contract and fees must be guaranteed for a minimum one-year time period. The contract may not be canceled by the TPA except in the case of nonpayment. Notice of termination or substantive change in the arrangement (including financial changes) must be given to *Employer A* at least 90 days prior to the end of the rate and contract guarantee.

Do you agree?   □ Yes   □ No   If no, note exceptions.

♦ **Legal representation:** *Employer A* reserves the right to select and/or approve legal representation for its disability cases.

Do you agree?   □ Yes   □ No   If no, note exceptions.

♦ **Hold harmless:** The selected TPA will not charge against experience those claim payments not authorized under the IDM plan if such payments were the result of error, negligence, reckless or willful acts, or omissions by the vendor, its agents or participants.

The TPA will indemnify and hold harmless *Employer A*, its agents, officers and employees from liability of any kind or nature (including costs, expenses or attorney fees) for damages suffered by any entity or person as a result of error, negligence, reckless or willful acts, or omissions of the vendor, its agents, officers or employers.

Do you agree?   □ Yes   □ No   If no, note exceptions.

PART II: REQUESTED ADMINISTRATIVE SERVICES

Claims Administration

Employer A is self-insured for workers' compensation and currently employs a TPA to review, adjudicate and manage all lost-time and medical-only workers' compensation claims for its (state) locations. *Employer A* seeks an ongoing administrative services relationship for an integrated disability claims management program in the following areas:

- ◆ Common intake center (toll-free number) for claims information
- ◆ Determination of compensability of all work-related claims within 14 days
- ◆ Consistent adjudication and management of accepted compensable lost-time WC claims and eligible STD and LTD claims
- ◆ Identification of subrogation opportunities on all potential claims where this could be a factor
- ◆ Identification of claims requiring investigation as well as field investigation services (such as surveillance) within three days of receipt or client request
- ◆ Determination and validation of all incurred expenses on a monthly basis
- ◆ Establishment within 14 days, and monthly updates thereafter, of the initial reserve level for ultimate exposure
- ◆ Application of principles of medical management of all claims either through internal or contracted services
- ◆ Provision of user-friendly *(Employer A-defined)* basic reports, on a monthly basis. These reports will provide the substance for monthly discussions and/or meetings with *Employer A.*
- ◆ Oversight, administration, and/or resolution of all *Employer A's* old open and run-out claims.

Prevention Services

The TPA must be willing and able to interface and work with *Employer A's* loss prevention and safety services vendor.

Managed Care Programs

Managed care services will be initiated and charged only when it is deemed necessary or appropriate and not for every reported injury/illness. Which of the following services does your organization provide?

- **Medical care management** that is consistent regardless of cause of injury or illness (occupational or nonoccupational)   ☐ Yes   ☐ No

- **Utilization review** for selected
  - –Inpatient hospital stays   ☐ Yes   ☐ No
  - –Outpatient services   ☐ Yes   ☐ No

    If yes, which ones? _____

    High-tech, high-cost diagnostic services (e.g., CT scan, MRI)   ☐ Yes   ☐ No
  - –Disability management   ☐ Yes   ☐ No

- **Medical bill review** with the following minimum expectations
  - –Usual and customary or fee adjustments schedule   ☐ Yes   ☐ No
  - –Appropriateness and relatedness   ☐ Yes   ☐ No
  - –Unbundling and upcoding   ☐ Yes   ☐ No

- **Hospital bill audit**   ☐ Yes   ☐ No

- **Preferred provider arrangements**   ☐ Yes   ☐ No

  If yes,
  - –What are the areas serviced?
  - –Do you lease or own the network?   ☐ Lease   ☐ Own
  - –Do you apply discounts for accessing the provider network?   ☐ Yes   ☐ No

  - –What is the usual percentage discount applied to individual providers and provider facilities? _____

PART III: CLAIMS EXPERIENCE

Plant Claims Experience

Average Number of Employees:

Year A _____

Year B _____

Year C _____

Year D _____

Year WC Claims Incurred:	*Number of Medical-Only Claims:*	*Number of Lost-Time Claims:*
Year A	_____	_____
Year B	_____	_____
Year C	_____	_____
Year D (1st 6 months)	_____	_____

Year Claims Incurred:	Number of STD Claims:	Number of LTD Claims:
Year A	_____	_____
Year B	_____	_____
Year C	_____	_____
Year D (1st 6 months)	_____	_____

Total Paid Costs

	Year A	Year B	Year C	Year D
Total medical	_____	_____	_____	_____
Medical-only claims	_____	_____	_____	_____
Lost-time claims	_____	_____	_____	_____
STD claims	_____	_____	_____	_____
LTD claims	_____	_____	_____	_____
Total indemnity	_____	_____	_____	_____
Total other (e.g., legal fees)	_____	_____	_____	_____

Old Open and Run-Out Claims

State	*Number of Claims*
State A	_____
Other applicable state	_____
Other applicable state	_____
Other applicable state	_____
Other applicable state	_____

Total Cost of Disability (Occupational and Nonoccupational)

Total Workers' Compensation Cost (U.S. Divisions)

	Year B *# Employees*	*Year B* *Cost*	*Year C* *# Employees*	*Year C* *Cost*
Hourly	_____	_____	_____	_____
Salaried	_____	_____	_____	_____
Total	_____	_____	_____	_____

Total Short-Term Disability Cost (U.S. Divisions)

	Year B *# Employees*	Year B *Cost*	Year C *# Employees*	Year C *Cost*
Hourly	_____	_____	_____	_____
Salaried	_____	_____	_____	_____
Total	_____	_____	_____	_____

Total Long-Term Disability Cost (U.S. Divisions)

	Year B *# Employees*	Year B *Cost*	Year C *# Employees*	Year C *Cost*
Hourly	_____	_____	_____	_____
Salaried	_____	_____	_____	_____
Total	_____	_____	_____	_____

PART IV: FINANCIAL FORMAT

Please provide a price quotation for each of the service areas on an unbundled basis. If discounts are available based on contracting for multiple services, this discount should also be indicated separately. Any cost not included in the per case or flat rate should be specifically identified. Do not deviate from the format provided; additional pages or footnotes may be provided if explanations are necessary.

Basic Claims Administration (for Life of Claim)

	Amount Per Case
Medical Only	$_____
Lost Time	$_____
STD	$_____
LTD	$_____
Old Open and Run-Out Claims	
♦ Oversight of WC claims	$_____
♦ Oversight of LTD claims	$_____
♦ Assumption of WC claims with intent to manage and/or close	$_____
♦ Assumption of LTD claims with intent to manage and/or close	$_____

Managed Care Program

	Option I Per Case	Option 2 Per Hour
Utilization Review		
♦ Inpatient	$_____	$_____
♦ Outpatient	$_____	$_____
♦ High-tech diagnostics	$_____	$_____
♦ Disability case management	$_____	$_____

If you provide disability case management services, are they owned or subcontracted by you? If subcontracted, through which company?

	Option I Percent Savings	Option 2 By Line
Medical Bill Review		
♦ Usual and customary	$_____	$_____
♦ Fee schedule compliance	$_____	$_____
♦ Appropriateness or relatedness	$_____	$_____
Hospital Bill Audit	$_____	$_____
Preferred Provider Arrangements (Per Employee Per Month)		$_____

Please specify any additional fees (e.g., start-up, Central Index Bureau, reports and meetings).

PART V: QUESTIONNAIRE

In responding to the questionnaire, please restate the question and then provide your written response. Your response to each question should not exceed one-half page.

General

1. What is the background and experience of your organization with respect to workers' compensation claims administration? With respect to STD claims administration? LTD? With respect to claims administration under an IDM program?

2. Please provide the following information regarding your market focus as of December 31, (year):

	Number of Contracts in Force	Number of Employees Covered	Last Year Premium/ Admin. Fees
Workers' Compensation			
♦ Insured	_____	_____	_____
♦ Self-Insured	_____	_____	_____
Group Health Plans			
♦ Insured	_____	_____	_____
♦ Self-Insured	_____	_____	_____
STD			
♦ Insured	_____	_____	_____
♦ Self-Insured	_____	_____	_____
LTD			
♦ Insured	_____	_____	_____
♦ Self-Insured	_____	_____	_____
IDM Program			
♦ Insured	_____	_____	_____
♦ Self-Insured	_____	_____	_____

3. Does your organization have service offices in (State)? If not, from which location will you service *Employer A's* account?

4. Do these offices have previous experience with IDM in *Employer A's* type of business? If yes, please specify which, and what size employee groups. If no, what will you do to become familiar with the claims experience and nuances of *Employer A's* business?

Managed Care

5. Please describe your managed care programs for the medical management of occupational and nonoccupational claims. Also note whether you purchased or contracted these service programs or developed them internally. Please specify if services are limited to a certain geographic area. The following should be addressed:
   - ◆ Utilization review
     - –Inpatient
     - –Outpatient
     - –High-tech diagnostics (MRI, CT scans, arthroscopy)
     - –Disability management
   - ◆ Bill review (review for usual and customary fees or compliance with state fee schedules, as well as appropriateness and relatedness of service to injury, upcoding and unbundling)
     - –Inpatient hospitalization bill audit
     - –Medical bill review
   - ◆ Preferred provider arrangements
   - ◆ Case/disability management services

6. Are you willing to unbundle these services for *Employer A?*

7. If the above programs are not in place, what plans, if any, are there to develop or purchase these programs or services for *Employer A?*

8. The exhibit at the end of this questionnaire outlines specific claims data requirements for a typical employer. Please indicate which elements are *not* captured by your IDM claims system.

Staffing

9. Please provide an organizational chart that illustrates the local claims office structure.

10. Who will be responsible for managing this account and where will this person be located? Provide a brief biography including the individual's education and years of experience in various assignments and the names of three similarly sized accounts the selected person currently represents.

11. What is the average caseload for your claims adjudication staff at any given time? Specify the average STD, LTD and WC caseloads. Within WC, what is the ratio of medical-only claims to lost-time claims?

12. If you have an IDM program in place, are adjusters cross-trained in the adjudication of STD, LTD and WC claims? If yes, what is their average caseload (specifying by claims type)? If no, is there a team approach to claims adjudication? Describe.

13. Please provide job descriptions that differentiate supervisor and senior- and junior-level adjusters' responsibilities.

14. What has been the turnover rate for the past two years for the claims-handling staff in the office that you propose for management of *Employer A's* account?

15. Please describe the clerical support of the proposed service office and the equipment and technology that is available (e.g., computers, software and fax).

16. Will there be a backup adjuster assigned to *Employer A's* account who will be knowledgeable in the event of turnover or leave of absence?

17. Do you have disability management nurses and/or physicians on staff to provide guidance and advice to the adjusters? Please describe their roles and responsibilities. If there are no clinical personnel on staff, how do adjusters obtain medical information clarification or support?

18. What training do claims staff receive prior to assuming a case load? Describe ongoing staff training and education as well as performance evaluation.

19. Please provide details on the qualifications and assigned workloads for the staff who will be assigned to this account. Do you anticipate hiring additional staff to service this account? Are you willing to add any necessary staff to meet the needs of *Employer A?*

Claims Processing

Integrated Occupational and Nonoccupational Claims System

20. Please provide the names of your current occupational and nonoccupational claims management system and whether it is owned by your organization or leased.

21. Are any major systems revisions expected during the next two years? If yes, please describe and define the potential impact on claims management services.

22. Are you willing to add any necessary staff to meet the needs of *Employer A.*

23. Does your system interface on line with the medical bill review function? If not, please describe interface procedures.

24. Describe the medical bill review service.

25. What database is used to determine UC&R limits? At what percentile of the UC&R scale do you generally adjust medical bills?

26. Does your medical bill review program detect and adjust bills for unbundling and upcoding? Is this an automated or manual process?

27. What is the turnaround time for the medical bill review process?

28. For the following claims paying functions, please categorize which of the three processing options (a-c) is used by your system:
    a. Claims processor determines from CRT screen
    b. Claims processor determines from paper files
    c. Computer systems determine
       −Verification of compensability
       −Relationship of medical bill to allowed condition
       −Duplicate bill check
       −Excessive services or fees
       −Possibility of third-party liability.

Claims Management

29. Do you have claims management practice standards? If yes, please include a copy. If not, are you willing to follow practice standards deemed necessary by Employer A (e.g., consistency and compliance with indemnity payments)?

30. Do you have criteria or guidelines in place for referral to case management, rehabilitation, independent medical examinations or other managed care services? If so, please provide. If not, how do you determine the need for these services?

31. If you have a case management program in place, do medical care services differ depending on the source of injury or illness (that is, occupational or nonoccupational)? If they presently differ, are you developing a more consistent practice? (If yes, describe your efforts.)

32. Do you maintain a list of specialty physicians? If so, how do you select them and evaluate their performance?

33. Discuss how you work with employers and medical providers to facilitate return to work.

34. Do you maintain three-point contact (employer, employee and medical provider) within 24 hours as an essential claims management criteria? If not, why not?

35. Describe your initial procedures for compensability determination (WC).

36. Describe your procedures for determining eligibility for STD. For LTD.

37. What procedures are in place to red flag medical-only claims that have potential to become lost-time claims?

38. Please describe how your claim files are maintained and organized (e.g., diary system, adjuster notes versus medical payment). Are claim files sorted on computer or hard copy? Can any claim file be obtained on the same day it is requested?

39. On average, how frequently do adjusters review their claim files? How often do supervisors do so, and how do they ensure that the adjusters follow up on their comments and recommendations? How are these reviews documented in the file?

40. How frequently do you provide status updates to your clients? What information is documented and provided at these meetings?

41. What steps does your company take to ensure prompt, accurate payment of compensation (indemnity) and medical bills?

42. Do you require medical reports prior to issuing medical bill payments?

43. Describe your internal fraud control procedures.

44. Describe your quality review procedures, including how claims are selected for this process and who conducts the review. Are results available to clients?

45. How long do you retain detailed claims information in your system?

46. How long do you maintain original claim documents?

47. Do you retain a copy of the actual claim on microfilm or microfiche? If so, please describe the entire archiving process.

48. List your security process for maintaining confidentiality of records.

49. Discuss your settlement practices with specific emphasis on the impact of (State) statutes.

50. *Employer A* is concerned about old open and run-out claims. Please describe actions your company would take in managing these claims to resolution or closure. Include advantages and disadvantages to acting in an oversight capacity versus assuming actual claims management responsibility.

Subrogation, Surveillance and Second-Injury Fund

51. Do you routinely provide subrogation services?

52. How do you identify claims with the potential for subrogation?

53. How do you routinely elicit information to determine the feasibility of accessing the second-injury fund?

54. How do you determine when to conduct claims investigation and surveillance? Please describe your available services as well as the criteria required to initiate these services.

Communication

55. Describe the telephone system utilized by your organization including, but not limited to, percent of calls per month receiving busy signals, availability of a 800 number and access to a live person as opposed to an electronic answering device.

56. Will you guarantee that all incoming calls from *Employer A* will be returned the same day they are placed?

57. Describe your standards and procedures for maintaining contact with the employer and employee. Provide timing of these contacts.

Reserving

58. What is your procedure for setting initial reserves for workers' compensation claims? What is the process for updating reserves? Please provide staff qualifications and specific experience. Describe your company's method of reserving for ultimate exposure.

59. Is documentation retained that justifies the original reserve amount and any subsequent adjustments? Please provide an example of how an adjustment is justified.

60. Do you audit your reserve accuracy? If so, what is your experience for the office you propose for *Employer A?*

Data Reporting and Analysis

61. Based on the proposal specifications, what standard reports would you generate for *Employer A?* With what frequency? Please describe and provide examples.

62. Is there one database for workers' compensation, short-term disability and long-term disability claims information?

63. Are reports integrated (i.e., supplying data for workers' compensation, short-term disability and long-term disability)?

64. What capabilities do you have to generate ad hoc reports? How do you charge for this service?

65. How often do you routinely meet with clients as a part of the contracted arrangement?

References

66. Please supply the names and phone numbers of three corporate references for whom you currently provide occupational and nonoccupational claims administration services and whose industry and size are similar to those of *Employer A*. The references should be assigned to your proposed service and claims office.

67. Please list your top three revenue-producing clients. Provide the name and phone number of the person at the company who best knows your service capabilities.

Other

68. What are your standard procedures for terminating an account? Do you maintain responsibility for open claims until they are closed, or do you transfer the responsibility to the new service organization? How do you forward files?

69. Discuss your excess loss arrangements relative to accounts such as *Employer A*.

70. Discuss your handling procedures for workers' compensation hearings. Please define roles and responsibilities of in-house resources versus outside legal counsel.

71. Please describe your safety and loss prevention services.

72. Please describe the banking options for bill payment that are available to *Employer A*.

73. Has the proposed local office of your organization ever been penalized for late payments or other statutory issues? If yes, please describe.

74. *Employer A* is interested in securing performance standards from its selected TPA. Please indicate your willingness to negotiate standards within the following areas. (This is not an all-inclusive list. Others may be added at contract time.)

    ☐ Initial review is completed within 24 hours of receipt.

    ☐ Compensability determination is made within 14 days.

    ☐ Contact is made with claimant, medical provider and *Employer A* within 48 hours of receipt of first report of injury.

    ☐ Initial indemnity payment is made within seven days of compensability determination and every 14 days thereafter, consistently. Accuracy with respect to right claimant, right amount and right date is 100% at all times.

    ☐ Reserve to ultimate cost is calculated within 90 days.

    ☐ Reserves compared to total payout are ±10%.

    ☐ Medical bill review and payment processes do not exceed ten days.

    ☐ A percentage of fees will be put at risk if agreed-upon performance standards are not met.

75. Please provide a copy of your annual report and most recent quarterly update. If unavailable, provide audited financial reports for (year) and (year).

76. Please provide a sample implementation outline and schedule that you would propose for *Employer A* to comply with a (month, day, year) start date.

Exhibit

CLAIM DATA REQUIREMENTS

Member/Patient Data

1. Patient identification
2. Age
3. Sex
4. Coverage code
5. Residential ZIP code
6. Birth date
7. Location
8. Division
9. Department
10. Job classification
11. Nature of injury
12. Cause of injury
13. Occupational or nonoccupational injury
14. Restricted duty duration
15. Disability duration
    a. Lost time
    b. Injury date through MMI date

Provider Data

16. Hospital name
17. Provider identification (tax ID number)
18. Provider type
    a. Hospital
    b. Physician (specialty code)
    c. Chiropractor
    d. Physical/occupational therapist
    e. Laboratory
    f. Psychiatric/chemical dependency treatment facility
    g. Dentist/oral surgeon
    h. Ph.D. (specialty)
    i. Surgeon (specialty)
    j. Nursing
    k. Extended care facility
    l. Outpatient surgery department
    m. Radiology
    n. Ambulance
    o. Home health care
    p. Optometrist
    q. Other

Service Type

19. Hospital
    a. ICU
    b. CCU
    c. Room and board
    d. Diagnostic x-ray and lab
    e. All others
20. Emergency room
21. Hospital outpatient (other than emergency room, x-ray and lab)
22. Extended care facility
23. Chemical dependency facility
24. Psychiatric facility
25. Outpatient surgical center
26. Professional fees, visits and number of procedures
    a. Inpatient surgery
    b. Outpatient surgery
    c. Inpatient physician visit
    d. Hospital outpatient physician visit
    e. Physician office and home visits
    f. Physician
    g. Chiropractor office visit
    h. Chiropractor x-ray
    i. Psychiatric office visit
    j. Psychiatric inpatient visit
    k. Anesthesiologist
    l. Home health care
    m. Radiologist inpatient
    n. Other
27. Nursing
28. Ambulance
29. Prescription drugs
30. Physical therapy, occupational therapy and work hardening
31. Outpatient lab
32. Outpatient x-ray
33. Nonhospital equipment and supplies (durable medical equipment)
34. Vision care (hardware)
35. All other

Data Required for All Service Types

36. Total billed charges
37. Eligible covered charges
38. Amount paid
39. Diagnostic code (ICD-9; hospital/professional)
40. DRG (if applicable)
41. Procedure code (CPT-4; professional services only)
42. Dates, number of visits, units, etc.
43. Treatment dates
44. Discharge diagnosis (ICD-9-CM)
45. Discharge status

Data Required for Inpatient Hospital Service

46. Date confined
47. Date discharged
48. Date of surgery
49. Admitting physician ID
50. Number of admissions this year
51. DRG/ICD-9 code

Payment Data

52. Billed charges
53. Eligible covered charges
54. UCR/fee schedule adjustments
55. Discounts (network)
56. Admitting physician ID
57. Duplicate payments
58. Subrogation
59. Benefits paid
60. Error ratios
61. Upcoding/unbundling

Appendix 6B

SCORE SHEET FOR SERVICE PROVIDER SELECTION

(Based on Answers to Sample Request for Proposal, Appendix 6A)

Service Provider's Name _____

Reviewer's Name _____

Overview

Category	Evaluation Criteria	Refers to RFP Section	Status (Basic expectations are in bold.)				Grade
			0	1	2	3	
Minimum Requirements	Agreed to all	Part I	No	Yes			
Integration Requirements	Intake	Part II	No	Yes			
	Medical mgmt.	Part II	No	Yes			
	RTW	Part V	No	Yes			
	Systems	Part V	No	Yes			
Questionnaire	Answered all	Part V	No	Yes			
Experience							
WC Experience	Number of years	Part V	< 2	2–5	6–15	> 15	
STD Experience	Number of years	Part V	< 2	2–5	6–15	> 15	

Service Provider's Name _____

Reviewer's Name _____

Category	Evaluation Criteria	Refers to RFP Section	Status (Basic expectations are in bold.)				Grade
			0	1	2	3	
LTD Experience	Number of years	Part V	< 2	2-5	6-15	> 15	
IDM Experience	Number of years	Part V	< 2	2-5	> 6		
Locations	Accessible service	Part V	No	Med. issues	**Min. issues**	In state	
Financial Stability	Based on Dunn and Bradstreet		No	Marginal	**Fine**		
Staffing							
Account Management Team • Quantity	Number of mgmt., technical, admin. and professional consultants	Part V	Too low	OK, but questionable ratio	Good		
• Quality	Experienced	Part V	None	Low	**Medium**	High	

Service Provider's Name _____

Reviewer's Name _____

Category	Evaluation Criteria	Refers to RFP Section	Status (Basic expectations are in bold.)				Grade
			0	1	2	3	
Trained Resources	Availability to claims adjusters or management team	Part V	None available	Level low or poor access	Level medium and good access	High	

Service Provider's Name _____

Reviewer's Name _____

Category	Evaluation Criteria	Refers to RFP Section	Status (Basic expectations are in bold.)				Grade
			0	1	2	3	
Adjuster Case Load (WC)	Best practices—Medical only (MO): 350 max. or Lost Time (LT): 150 max. or MO:50-75 and LT: 75 max.	Part V	High	**Fair**	Best practice		
Adjuster Case Load (STD)	Best practices	Part V	High	**Fair**	Best practice		

Service Provider's Name _____

Reviewer's Name _____

Category	Evaluation Criteria	Refers to RFP Section	Status (Basic expectations are in bold.)				Grade
			0	1	2	3	
Adjuster Case Load (LTD)	Best practices	Part V	High	**Fair**	Best practice		
Adjuster Case Load (IDM)	Best practices— For team: see levels for WC, STD and LTD; Cross-trained adjuster load:	Part V	High	**Fair**	Best practice		
Staff Turnover	Rate	Part V	High	**Medium**	Low		

Service Provider's Name _____

Reviewer's Name _____

Category	Evaluation Criteria	Refers to RFP Section	Status (Basic expectations are in bold.)				Grade
			0	1	2	3	
Staff Training	Initial and ongoing	Part V	None for one or both	Low	**Medium**	High	
Current Practices							
Common Claims Intake	Does or can	Part V	No	Can	**Does**		
Integrated Reporting	Does or can	Part V	No	Can	**Does**		
Return to Work	Early, production RTW procedures	Part V	No program	Basic	**Moderate**	Best practices	

Service Provider's Name _____

Reviewer's Name _____

Category	Evaluation Criteria	Refers to RFP Section	Status (Basic expectations are in bold.)				Grade
			0	1	2	3	
Communication • Employee	Within 24 hours; regularly	Part V	None	Within 48 hours	Within 24 hours and regularly		
• Physician	Within 24 hours; regularly	Part V	None	Within 48 hours	Within 24 hours and regularly		
• Employer	Within 24 hours; regularly and when triggered	Part V	None	Within 48 hours	Within 24 hours, regularly and when triggered		

Service Provider's Name _____

Reviewer's Name _____

Category	Evaluation Criteria	Refers to RFP Section	Status (Basic expectations are in bold.)				Grade
			0	1	2	3	
Medical Care Management • Direction	Guide to qualified medical providers	Part V	No	Yes	Guide and clinically monitor	Best practice	
• Consistent occupational and non-occupational illness/injury	Quality, consistent medical care management independent of injury/illness cause	Part V	No	Yes, consistent	Consistent, high quality		
Current and Future Info and Reporting	Capacity and flexibility	Part V	None	Poor	**Medium**	Best practice	

Service Provider's Name _____

Reviewer's Name _____

Category	Evaluation Criteria	Refers to RFP Section	Status (Basic expectations are in bold.)				Grade
			0	1	2	3	
Proper Utilization of Attorney	Balance between attorney and case manager	Part V	Attorney totally responsible	Case mgr. responsible	Balance of case mgr. and attorney		
Legal Resources	Legal staff, outside agency	Part V	None	Staff			
Subrogation Process	Established process, subrogation unit	Part V	Neither	Process	Process and unit		
Procedures to Pursue Funds/ Second Injury	Documented procedure and staff	Part V	Neither	Documented procedure	Documented procedure and staff		

Service Provider's Name _____

Reviewer's Name _____

Category	Evaluation Criteria	Refers to RFP Section	Status (Basic expectations are in bold.)				Grade
			0	1	2	3	
Reserving	Methodology	Part V	None	Questionable	Adequate		
Quality Review	Written procedures with documented measurements and followup	Part V	None	Basic	Good	Best practice	
Quality Standards	Documented	Part V	Below minimum	Minimum	Moderate	Best practice	
Fraud Detection	Controls and review department	Part V	No plan	Plan	Specialized department		

Service Provider's Name _____

Reviewer's Name _____

Category	Evaluation Criteria	Refers to RFP Section	Status (Basic expectations are in bold.)				Grade
			0	1	2	3	
Experience with new ideas such as absence management	Innovation		No	Low	Medium	High	
	Flexibility		No	Low	Medium	High	
Total	Basic Expectations =						Pass -or- Fail

Service Provider's Name _____

Reviewer's Name _____

Client References

List three clients with number of employees similar to Employer A.

Category	Refers to	Comments	Grade
Company:	Part V		
Contact:			
Phone:			
Company:			
Contact:			
Phone:			
Company:			
Contact:			
Phone:			
Total			

Service Provider's Name _____

Reviewer's Name _____

List the three top revenue producing clients.

Category	Refers to	Comments	Grade
Company:	Part V		
Contact:			
Phone:			
Company:			
Contact:			
Phone:			
Company:			
Contact:			
Phone:			
Total			

Service Provider's Name _____

Reviewer's Name _____

Financial Profile

Financial stability, quoted fees and costs related to training materials, reports, travel and other related expenses should be included. Fees must be quoted in the format request in Part IV.

Annual reports (financial stability) were submitted and reviewed?   ☐ Yes   ☐ No.

Appendix 6C

REFERENCE QUESTIONS

1. How long has _____ been your service provider? How many offices service your account? Do you notice any difference between these offices?

2. What do you like best about _____?

3. What do you like least about _____?

4. Does _____ provide a single source for intake for occupational and nonoccupational claims?

5. Does _____ use the same medical provider for occupational and nonoccupational disability management?

6. Does _____ manage return to work consistently regardless of origin (occupational/nonoccupational) of injury or illness?

7. Have you been satisfied with the day-to-day service? The account team?

8. Has _____ been flexible in meeting your company's specific requests?

9. Does _____ respond promptly to your inquiries?

10. Was _____ willing to take over old claims from your previous service provider? How did this go?

11. Have your employees been satisfied with the timeliness of payments, as well as _____'s responsiveness to any questions?

12. Have you noticed any increase or decrease in the number of employee complaints?

13. Does _____ provide you with meaningful and understandable reports to monitor claims experience, utilization patterns, program savings? Are reports timely?

14. Are the reports you receive from _____ integrated?

15. Are reports useful to tracking, trending, forecasting, problem solving?

16. Does _____ go over reports with you on a regular or as-needed basis?

17. How often do you meet with the vendor?

18. Do you feel _____ is reasonably priced? Have fee increases been reasonable? Any hidden costs?

19. Would you recommend _____ to other employers?

I DM can be a huge step forward for employers. It improves both quality and employee satisfaction and reduces cost. However, no matter how brilliantly conceived, the program will fail to reach its full potential unless all stakeholders understand their roles and responsibilities, and unless good behavior is rewarded and bad behavior is punished. (See Exhibit 7A: Obstacles to Implementation.) It is, therefore, essential to develop a detailed implementation plan that includes communication methods and incentives for adopting desired behavior changes.

Chapter 7

Successfully Implementing an IDM Program

by Nancy C. Qutub

To determine readiness for an IDM program, the employer assembles a team to assess the current state of the company's disability claims processes, disability costs, productivity and data accessibility. This team also outlines the benefits and obstacles to initiating an IDM program and recommends a plan of action.[1] When an employer decides to adopt an IDM program, gears shift. The assessment team becomes the implementation team by retaining appropriate members and adding employee and communication department representatives. Using the assessment checklist as a starting point, the implementation team revisits components discussed earlier, and thoroughly identifies, prioritizes and communicates relevant issues. While the previous assessments were made to determine whether IDM is a reasonable choice for the employer, the implementation team's fine-tuning ranks goals and

Exhibit 7A

OBSTACLES TO IMPLEMENTATION

creates "the message for change." It directs the structure of an employer's IDM program–including partnerships and communication methods–and the implementation time frame. In addition, the team verifies personnel and other resource requirements, and outlines and begins necessary training. It joins all the pieces together to create a unified approach to managing disability.

Goals and the Message

The Reasons for Change

To increase support for its IDM program, a company develops a message that explains both the reasons for change and the potential benefits. An employer that decides to implement a new program has some unmet goals. While these overall goals may differ from one company to another, more likely it is their priority that varies. Regardless of what they are, however, goals and objectives are the reasons for change; and because change makes demands–often costly in time or money or individual comfort– the reasons need to be perceived as worth the effort.

For the majority of companies, the reasons for change include lowering costs, increasing productivity, and attaining data useful in program measurement and the development of risk and prevention strategies. Each of the broad goals has associated objectives, which should become part of the message as well.

Exhibit 7B shows examples of goals and associated objectives.

Support for the Message

In developing a message based on input from all groups (as it would be with an assessment/implementation team approach), an employer promotes support for changes. But to emphasize the importance of these changes and the company's commitment to them requires action from top executives. Executives must back the initiatives by their words and actions or the company's commitment to change is halfhearted.

Once its message has been clearly formed and support amassed, the task becomes one of structuring a program that accommodates company goals, culture and assets.

Structure of the IDM Program

Company Variables

In trying to determine the best structure for its IDM program, an employer becomes introspective. While not an exhaustive list (see "IDM

Exhibit 7B

THE MESSAGE

Goals	Measurable Objectives
Lowering costs	• Administrative savings: nonduplication of forms, more effective use of claims personnel • Discovery and elimination of duplicate claims • "Sports medicine" approach to injury that often shortens medical treatment time (reducing medical costs) and time off work • Decrease in the cost of replacement personnel and overtime • Reduced litigation
Increasing productivity	• Management efficiency (jobs covered with trained people) • Decrease in hours worked by untrained, temporary personnel and full-time employees who do their work and cover for absent coworkers • Satisfaction with the quality and delivery of health care • Increased participation in prevention and wellness programs (employees healthier and better able to perform their jobs) • Awareness that the company appreciates its employees • Greater customer (employee) satisfaction
Attaining data useful for program measurement and the development of risk and prevention strategies	• Nonoccupational and occupational claims information in one database • Integrated reporting

Assessment Checklist" in Appendix 5A for a complete list), the following areas influence the design of a company's program:

◆ Size and location(s)
◆ Industry
◆ Unionization
◆ Employee turnover
◆ Fiscal status
◆ Corporate culture
  –Recent experience with change
  –Flexibility
  –Management style (autocratic, paternal, decentralized, etc.)
◆ Employee demographics
  –Age
  –Gender
  –Ethnicity
  –Race
  –Primary language
  –Job position
  –Length of service.

IDM Program Elements

With goals and company variables in the foreground, an employer determines which of the following elements are essential to its program:

◆ Integrated claims management (common intake for claims and, possibly, claims adjusters who are cross-trained in the handling of occupational and nonoccupational claims)
◆ Integrated medical care management (early clinical intervention, physical rehabilitation and provider networks or individual providers employing return-to-work practices)
◆ Consistent return-to-work program (light duty or job modification regardless of cause of injury or illness)
◆ Integrated information systems (online access to claims data and integrated data for outcomes management; near real-time exchange of information between case managers and medical providers)[2]
◆ Safety, prevention and wellness programs (programs that address company experience and employee demographics).

Implementation Approach

To decide the appropriate implementation approach, the employer considers not only the company variables and elements outlined above but also which components are already present within the company and the current state of those components: established and essential; worthwhile but underused; or ineffectual or counterproductive. Weighing all these pieces, the employer chooses one of the following approaches to implementation:

◆ Partial: While all the components of an IDM program will not be achieved, the employer chooses to integrate one or more areas.

◆ Phased: The employer will implement completely an IDM program, but in stages based on what assets it already possesses, as well as its primary goal.

◆ Simultaneous and complete: This approach may be most feasible for an employer that has some of the elements already in place. For example, a company currently having an information system with one database for all claims is ahead of many of its competitors. It may be able to coordinate the complete and simultaneous implementation of an IDM program.

No matter which overall approach a company chooses, the team outlines the steps and gathers the resources necessary for attaining those steps, assigns responsibilities and establishes the time frame for putting the components in place.

Partnerships

The structure of an IDM program demands specific partnerships. While it is important for an employer to choose the right vendor or provider (refer to Chapters Four and Six for discussions of the partner selection), all partnerships require continual nurturing. An employer supports successful partnerships through shared goals, assigned responsibilities and authority, appropriate training, incentives and ongoing assessment.

Shared Goals

How do the efforts of the employer, employees, insurance carrier or third-party administrator and health care providers mesh? What makes the successful combination of individual contributions important to all participants? Partners value program accomplishment when they understand the individual benefits that spring from shared success. When partners view their sacrifice of time or autonomy or initial monetary gain as worth the benefits reaped under integration, cooperation grows. An employer promotes such growth by communicating well, by respecting various perspectives and giving them voice, and by reporting measurable results. (See the communication section of this chapter.)

Responsibilities and Authority

Defined responsibilities and areas of authority encourage accountability and prevent duplication of effort. A list that includes all the partners, their responsibilities and objectives clarifies the performance expected from each partner in an integrated program. As an example, Exhibit 7C outlines the communication responsibilities for a workers' compensation injury.

In a similar manner, the implementation team lists each partner's responsibilities—with an accompanying time frame when appropriate—for every aspect of integration where individuals are held accountable. Given the means and authority to act in a manner to fulfill their separate responsibilities, the partners must also realize how these pieces fit together to reach shared goals.

Training[3]

Complementing their new responsibilities within an IDM program is the training that enables the partners to do their jobs well. For the most part, training under IDM implies the education of plan administrators, supervisors and managers, health care providers, care managers and TPAs, and insurance carriers (claims management, claims assistants, bill processors and customer service). In a vertically integrated program, however, the department(s) in charge of employee safety and health will be trained to stress proactive measures, as will the employees themselves.

An employer has the following basic training objectives for all the partners:

- ◆ To merge the competencies of the present operations with the knowledge and best practices underlying IDM
- ◆ To design learning experiences that are team and practice oriented but meet the needs of specific partners
- ◆ To produce a formal training program that can be evaluated to determine accuracy and validity of content and efficiency of teaching methods.

In order to meet these objectives, an employer determines the partners' present capabilities and knowledge of IDM and then develops the training methods to move participants from a nonintegrated way of doing things to a fully integrated one. Exhibit 7D lists areas in which training is commonly required, the participants and the suggested training

Exhibit 7C

COMMUNICATION RESPONSIBILITIES IN A WORKERS' COMPENSATION INJURY[1]

Partner	Stage			
	Pre-Injury	Injury	Ongoing Care	Return to Work
Company Management	Establishes communication lines, procedures and methods. Informs other partners about procedures.	Ensures that procedures are followed.	Receives and tracks outcomes.	Provides, adjusts appropriately, and publicizes light-duty jobs.
Communication Department[2]	Helps determine the means and methods of communication and facilitates efforts throughout the company and between partners. Is held accountable for the overall quality of communication.	Helps determine the means and methods of communication and facilitates efforts throughout the company and between partners. Is held accountable for the overall quality of communication.	Helps determine the means and methods of communication and facilitates efforts throughout the company and between partners. Is held accountable for the overall quality of communication.	Helps determine the means and methods of communication and facilitates efforts throughout the company and between partners. Is held accountable for the overall quality of communication.
Risk Manager (Safety) and Human Resources Department (Wellness)	Establish safety procedures and wellness programs and publicize them through posters, handouts, meetings, etc.	Track numbers, types and causes of injuries. Develop and communicate safety or prevention programs based on this information.		Help develop and communicate job accommodations that incorporate safety and wellness best practices. Communicate accident information that would lead to better safety procedures.

1. In the "Findings" from the *CIGNA Integrated Care/Gallup Survey of Employee Experience with Disability and the Benefit Process*, April 1998 (p. 7), communication and return-to-work programs are critically linked: "A surprising finding was nearly two out of three workers surveyed (61%) said no one had discussed their return-to-work plans with them while they were away from work. This percentage jumps to 72% among workers who reported their employer did not have a return-to-work program. This suggests how important communication and commitment are to the overall return-to-work process."

2. If there is no communication department within the company, the implementation team assigns the role and responsibilities to some other entity. An individual or group must be held accountable for the coordination and overall quality of communication efforts, which cannot be left to chance.

Exhibit 7C (Continued)

COMMUNICATION RESPONSIBILITIES IN A WORKERS' COMPENSATION INJURY

Partner	Stage			
	Pre-Injury	Injury	Ongoing Care	Return to Work
Supervisor	Encourages open communication with employees.	Knows procedures for work injury; notifies person responsible for FROI filing.	Contacts employee just to ask how he is doing.[3]	Communicates with employee, case manager and safety department. Offers job placement when appropriate.
Employee	Is aware of safety procedures.	Reports injury promptly to call center or supervisor. Goes to provider when warranted; communicates pertinent health information.	Contacts employer about absence. Understands provider's instructions, adheres to them and brings concerns to his attention.	Contacts employer about return to work.
Health Care Provider	Knows communication procedures for this employer.	Details injury and prognosis; develops care plan with employee and care manager.	Relays treatment plan to care manager; consults with employer or care manager about light-duty or regular job demands. Speaks with patient about RTW.	Signs release for employee's return to work. Notifies care manager.
TPA/Insurance Carrier/ Care Manager	Knows and follows communication procedures for this employer.	Contacts provider and employee to ascertain extent of injury and prognosis; develops care plan with provider and employee.	Communicates at contracted intervals (within 24 hours of injury notification, after doctor's visit, every two weeks, etc.) with employee, provider and employer.	Contacts employer about doctor's release; talks with employee about his return to work.

3. The employer should consider the conflicting opinions on supervisor/employee communication before establishing a particular policy. Some companies argue that when the supervisor does not contact the injured employee, the employee feels no one cares. Isolated, he is less likely to return to work quickly. Other companies believe when a supervisor calls, the employee feels unfairly pressured to return to work before he is physically ready.

Exhibit 7D

IDM TRAINING TABLE

TRAINING	PARTICIPANTS	SUGGESTED METHODS
Introduction to IDM, which includes a historical perspective, terminology, models, primary roles and responsibilities, and the critical elements of service	• Plan administrator • Risk manager (safety) • Human resources (benefits, wellness program) • Supervisor/manager • Health care provider • TPA/insurance carrier • Clinical care manager • Communications department (Divide participants into knowledge-based groups and focus lecture accordingly.)	• Classroom lecture followed by discussion • Printed material including definitions and models • Responsibility flowcharts
Integrated Case Management	• Plan administrator • Health care provider • TPA/insurance carrier • Clinical care manager	• Classroom lecture followed by discussion • Case study • Role playing
Administrative requirements for WC claims	• Plan administrator • TPA/insurance carrier	• Classroom lecture followed by discussion • Case study • Role playing
Administrative requirements for STD and LTD claims	• Plan administrator • TPA/insurance carrier	• Classroom lecture followed by discussion • Case study • Role playing
Common claims intake	• Plan administrator • TPA/insurance carrier • Call center personnel (if not TPA/insurance carrier)	• Classroom lecture followed by discussion • Role playing

methods. The employer's job is to pick the best methods for the subject and audience.

Behavior Change and the Use of Incentives[4]

Changing behavior, even after people have been trained correctly, is difficult. Without incentives, behavior change is unlikely. Incentives provide the impetus for change by answering the "What's in it for me?" question.

Exhibit 7D (Continued)

IDM TRAINING TABLE

TRAINING	PARTICIPANTS	SUGGESTED METHODS
Integrated approach to return to work	• Plan administrator • Risk manager (safety) • Human resources (benefits, wellness program) • Supervisor/manager • Health care provider • Clinical care manager	• Classroom lecture followed by discussion • Case study • Role playing • Tour of work facilities
Integrated computer systems	• Plan administrator • Health care provider (if information is transferred online) • TPA/insurance carrier • Clinical care manager • Communications department	• Classroom lecture followed by discussion • Printed software material • Hands-on practice
Primary prevention	• Plan administrator • Risk manager (safety) • Human resources (benefits, wellness program) • Supervisor/manager • On-site medical staff • Health care provider • Communications department • Employee	• Classroom lecture (the role prevention plays in an IDM program) followed by discussion • Safety videos • Disease-specific pamphlets • Demonstration video or class for exercise programs

Having determined what behavioral changes it wants to target (such as increased support from medical providers for the company's RTW programs or healthier employee exercise habits), the implementation team should propose incentives that will increase the likelihood of success. The following suggestions may guide the team's decisions:

◆ Keep design as simple as possible. Anything that is not understood has no value.

◆ Start with less expensive approaches. A company is better served by increasing the value of incentives rather than by taking anything away.

◆ When a company mixes cash and noncash incentives it creates more vitality in its incentives program. Also, by designing both individual and group awards, a company can balance individual and team goals.

◆ The dollar amount of incentives does not have to be great. If incentives are developed, modified and enhanced with the participation from those targeted and if they are communicated effectively, amounts as little as $50 can actually promote behavioral change.

◆ Incentives should be at least self-funding. That is, incentives should generate sufficient revenues, savings and/or productivity to pay for themselves. Establish an estimated return on investment (tested and validated) to determine the potential value of proposed incentives.

◆ As their impact tends to shift over time, assess incentives frequently; they should become neither entitlements nor "nothing-much." Limit the time a specific incentive is in effect, switch tactics (individual versus group incentives, for example) or re-publicize an incentive that seems underused but still somewhat successful.

◆ Publicize success and ensure that senior management is involved in linking incentives to business strategy, in measuring their success and in delivering them to those who have earned them. This will greatly increase their perceived value.

The use of incentives, often necessary for a program's success, is also attractive because it can be customized to encourage specific behavior, to reach groups or individuals and to cover a variety of time spans as well as a mix of rewards. The examples that follow illustrate this diversity:

◆ A large Midwestern manufacturing company introduced a gain-sharing plan in two of its plants. In addition to increasing output, the company wanted to increase productivity through reducing absence and injury. Goals for a 20% reduction were jointly established and gains were shared on an equal basis between the company and workers. Absence decreased 22% and work-related, reported injuries dropped by 25%.

◆ In 1997, the city of Asheville, North Carolina, "waived the participating employees' co-payments for insulin and supplies as an incentive for them to enroll in the program [a six-month pilot diabetes management program]."[5] Coached by pharmacists on a monthly basis about their medication and the data from their blood sugar monitor, "these individuals [program participants] were taking better care of themselves than they had in years, in terms of diet, sleep, exercise–in every regard."[6] As a result of its success, this program has become a permanent part of the benefits plan and a similar program has been started that targets asthma.

◆ Another employer, worried about absenteeism, communicated (through newsletters, posters and a video) the impact absenteeism was having on the employees' pension plan. Working with the union for over a year-and-a-half, this employer developed a new absence management policy: each employee receives five free sick days per year; however, he is credited 20 hours of pay for perfect attendance, with four hours deducted for each day off.[7]

◆ Hormel Food Corporation has a yearly group travel incentive. "At the beginning of each year a set of criteria is given to each employee in every department, highlighting their goals for the year, whether it is lost-time management, reducing injuries or improving performance levels." Thirty-six employees and their spouses are picked by management based on employees' performance against the criteria.[8]

While the use of incentives promotes and energizes activity, it also compels caution on the part of the initiator. Evaluate the program's success carefully. If, for example, a manager or department misrepresents its safety records so that it can look good or win an incentive, the goal is lost. In such cases, it might be better to focus on behavior (Are more people wearing back braces or ear plugs? Are the floors clean when surprise inspections occur?) than on the reported number of accidents.

Assessment of Partnerships

As it evaluates incentives, so, too, must the employer assess partnerships. These assessments may be formal (for example, a claims audit) or casual (the daily tally of health center participation). In either case, the steps for assessing the various partnerships remain the same:

◆ Determine what is expected of successful partnerships.
◆ Decide what data needs to be collected to ascertain performance level.
◆ Settle on the methods (and time frame) for data collection.
◆ Collect and transfer the data to the party responsible for analysis.
◆ Analyze the data.
◆ Communicate the results; discuss changes that need to be made and initiate them.

Because it is not only the connections but also the quality of each of the pieces that determines the overall success of an integrated system, assessing partnerships is important, and locating bottlenecks is crucial.

In some cases, statistical feedback may be enough to encourage change, but in others the employer may need to enforce consequences for failing to support the IDM program.

Communication

There may be no other factor as important to the overall success of a company's IDM program as communication. Especially during implementation, communication either bonds components into a cohesive program or, if inadequate, fosters disjointed parts.

Early and Interactive Communication

If they are not informed accurately and early in the process (at the point where changes are being considered), employees/unions, health care providers and insurance vendors learn independently about proposed changes to disability benefits. Rumor creates partial truths–slanted in the retelling by biases–and a barrier that is hard to undo.[9] To prevent this unnecessary obstacle, a company teams with the affected groups (forming the integration team) as early in the process as possible.

Starting with the overall importance of an IDM program to the company, the team lists the groups involved in the program and how the changes affect them. A detailed and painstakingly honest approach to necessary adjustments and expected benefits spurs program acceptance. Later, messages geared for individual groups will stem from this list, but perhaps the greater benefit is the increased understanding between team members and the recognition given various perspectives.

Recognizable Message

It would be helpful if, like an advertising firm, the team creates a slogan to punctuate the message. This slogan or tag line, specific to the company and its primary goal(s), becomes easily recognizable and readily associated with the program. A tag line affords the integration team another opportunity to encapsulate the message. Examples follow:
- ◆ Our IDM Program Works for Employees
- ◆ IDM: Prevention, Care and Return to Health
- ◆ IDM Supports Health.

Frequent and Timely Communication

Communication, started early in the process and readily associated with the program, becomes even more effective when the team considers its timetable. Certainly notification, including such things as responsibilities and requirements, accompanies each of the stages of implementation. Communication efforts continue, however, when the program is established. During new employee orientation and when an employee changes benefits, the company highlights its program. Publicity for specific components can piggyback on related promotions, while brochures are prepared and later distributed to employees when a threatened or actual absence due to illness or injury occurs.

The frequency of communication varies according to what is being publicized. If, for example, one of the major components of a company's integrated program is employee wellness efforts, then such things as health screening, exercise programs and smoking cessation classes suggest the appropriateness of frequent, appealing and varied communication.

Multiple Communication Methods

The variety of communication methods offers opportunity as well as challenge. A company, mindful of its communication budget, weighs cost, availability and effectiveness of the various methods. Aware that people respond individualistically to the sundry forms of communication, an employer exercises more than one means to inform them whenever possible.

In deciding which methods (written, electronic and face-to-face communication) to use to convey its message, a company considers the following:
- ◆ Cost
- ◆ Audience
- ◆ Access of the audience to the means of communication
- ◆ Appropriateness of method
  - −Permanency of the message
  - −Time frame for conveying the message
  - −Appeal.

Written Communication

Written communication is often the method of choice, and in some cases written notification is required by law. Written communication encompasses everything from annual reports to posters to payroll stuffers. It includes in-house newsletters or insurance company publications sent to employees' homes with such information as cholesterol-lowering diets or exercise for backaches; departmental flyers that announce intramural sports or safety records or health fairs; new employee brochures that explain the IDM program in detail; and wallet cards printed with instructions for emergencies.

When an employee is injured or becomes ill, the requirements, roles and expectations are often communicated to him in written detail, but in addition an outline of step-by-step obligations (including whom and where to call, what information to compile, and what other actions to take) should be available at all times to supervisors and workers throughout the company.

No matter which written forms it uses, the employer needs to keep in mind the audience. If printed communication buries staff desks or if many of the workers are illiterate in English, the written word loses much of its value.

Electronic Communication

Many companies are turning to electronic communication, especially for messages that change often, need rapid conveyance, or seldom require a hard copy. This includes e-mail and web pages; online computer links among employer, provider and claims management; video and in-house television; and interactive voice response systems.

In companies where most employees have access to computers, e-mail and web pages are frequently preferred. E-mail messages update employees quickly and encourage prompt feedback, and web pages can easily advertise safety or wellness initiatives. Both serve as an administrative hot line for off-site employees and other partners who have appropriate computer access.

Although costly at first glance, employer/provider/insurance vendor computer links can lessen paperwork and reporting time and promote accuracy (with less manual transfer of information). The ability to do this is one of the major reasons for partnering with a specific provider group or claims administrator. Without it, integrated management is limited.

Videos enable an employer to offer detailed information on a host of topics (such as alleviating back pain, ergonomics in the workplace and safety procedures for specific office or factory equipment). If a company must ensure that a large number of immigrant workers understand its new program or procedures, it can produce an in-house video with the help of a bilingual employee. Videos work equally well for those individuals who learn visually, for group discussions that require those present to receive the same information and for individuals who cannot attend a group meeting.

Likewise, an interactive voice response system may be used for many purposes:[10]

- To announce short messages such as time, date, location of meetings or programs
- To announce individual status of days off or claim progress
- To allow for activity, program or benefits registration
- To allow for change in registration
- To allow for absence notification, request for substitute worker
- To allow for the request for general health or disease-specific information
- To allow for prescription renewal
- To allow 24-hour access to all of the above options.

Face-to-Face Communication

While written and electronic communications are the methods often used to convey change, face-to-face dialogues remain important. The form varies according to the purpose, the audience and the type of information. Corporate seminars or on-site speakers relay information to large audiences but sometimes discourage the exchange of ideas or fail to address individual concerns. In contrast, departmental meetings—in which the individuals responsible for implementing a new program meet with small groups of employees—are more effective in recognizing department-specific issues. Town hall meetings with their question and answer character provide a similar exchange for the entire company or location.

Assessment of Communication

Assess communication efforts. If communication is successful, awareness and the appropriate use of the integrated program increase. To measure communication's effectiveness, a company first considers what information is useful. Are employees and providers aware of job accommodations? Are more employees using the wellness center? Do employees with chronic conditions consult in-house medical staff? Do claims administrators get appropriate and timely information from the employer and the provider? Do employees out on disability receive communication from their supervisors? Do they feel the company wants them to return to work?

Second, the company decides which assessment methods to use. In addition to audits and informal tallies, surveys supply quantitative data; interviews and focus groups encourage longer, more qualitative answers. On the one hand, survey questions such as, "When you were off the job on workers' compensation, how many times did your supervisor contact you?" and "What were the topics of these conversations?" can provide specific data. Focus groups and interviews, on the other hand, allow for the collection of longer, subjective comments to such questions as: "Describe your company's wellness program. How would you improve it?" or "Has communication between your office (the provider) and the employer changed since integration? How? What recommendations for improving communication do you have?"

By gathering and analyzing the data, an employer learns which communication efforts work and which need improvement. It can then refine communication so the IDM components work together seamlessly.

Summary

After deciding to initiate an IDM program, the employer forms an implementation team. This team identifies the components necessary to promote company goals and business strategy as they relate to disability management; it augments or replaces the employer's resources to meet the requirements for these components; and, through aggressive communication practices, the team meshes the components and resources into a seamless IDM program.

Endnotes

1. The IDM assessment team includes vendor and provider representatives as well as knowledgeable individuals from the departments responsible for executing disability programs. See Chapter Five: "Assessing Readiness for IDM" for a complete team description. Refer to the "IDM Assessment Checklist," Appendix 5A.

2. See "Privacy Concerns" in Chapter Four for legal issues that may arise from an integrated information system.

3. Sharon E. Muran, a clinical instructor at the University of Illinois at the Medical Center, developed the IDM Training Table and much of the training information incorporated in this section. A registered nurse with a master's degree in public health, Ms. Muran is an executive IDM consultant for Marsh Risk Consulting.

4. Claudia Wyatt-Johnson supplied most of the thoughts on incentives as well as the example of the Midwestern company and its gain-sharing initiative. For 20 years, Ms. Wyatt-Johnson (co-founder of Partners In Performance, Chicago, IL) has been helping clients achieve competitive advantage through design and implementation of strategic human resource programs. Her primary emphasis is the design of reward programs to support business strategy. Ms. Wyatt-Johnson has master's degrees in political science and industrial relations from Loyola University.

5. Robert Kazel, "Benefit Beat: Disease Management Success Prompts Second Program," *Business Insurance,* 30 March 1998, 6.

6. Ibid.

7. Sonja Felix, "Putting Attendance on the Right Track," *Benefits Canada,* June 1998.

8. Joan M. Steinauer, "Motivation 101," *How to Run an Incentive Program,* http://www. incentivemag.com/news/billcomm.htm, October 26, 1998.

9. Stressing the importance of communication to a company, Kathy Simmons (in "Qualities of World-Class Managers," *The Economics Press Daily Motivator,* http://www.epinc.com/stories/page2htm, October 26, 1998) wrote, "Most problems in business can be traced back to poor or nonexistent communication. Why is this so common? Because it takes ongoing effort that many managers aren't willing to expend. You can either give 100% effort in this area or be at peace with the fact that your employees will use valuable company time trying to figure out what is going on. Be warned, however: If you choose the latter, people will resent being uninformed and productivity will decrease even further. The saying 'There's never too much communication' is quite true in today's fast-changing business arena. Communication is an area in which you cannot afford to be slack."

10. Check for translation services available through the phone companies if your employees require voice mail messages in languages other than English.

As IDM leaves its infancy, the problem of how to measure its success takes on critical importance. There are, however, two major factors universally accepted as determinants of a successful IDM program: decreased costs and increased employee satisfaction.

Chapter 2 discussed numerous variations to the basic concepts of IDM. Some definitions focus on funding mechanisms; others on management techniques; but, regardless of the definition, each has a dramatic effect on program design and outcome. Additionally, consideration must be given to the characteristics of the environment in which an employer implements an integrated program. Company size, existing benefits, current program costs, industry classification and geographic location are a few of the environmental factors that can affect the program's makeup. While a service provider may offer a so-called off-the-shelf program, the very nature of both the service provider and the client will add an element of uniqueness to the program and its subsequent outcomes.

Given these various nuances, it is essential that employers looking to integrate develop a means to evaluate their programs in order to benchmark against their own past experience, other programs and the projections of service providers.[1] A program that produces a 25% savings in the total cost of disability for one employer may not achieve the same results for another. The only

Chapter 8
Program Evaluation Basics for IDM

by Keith M. Higdon

true savings are those the employer or service provider measures and compares against program costs, although a program that achieves dramatic cost reduction at the expense of employee satisfaction cannot be described as successful.

In order to appropriately measure outcomes, the evaluation process must begin at the inception of a program and continue throughout its development. The development of an integrated program has at least four phases:

◆ Design
◆ Implementation
◆ Management
◆ Outcomes.

While *outcomes* represent the fourth phase of development, their measurement is an integral part of the three preceding phases. More than a retrospective analysis, a thorough evaluation involves connecting design and implementation with the outcomes observed. An evaluation that is itself designed and implemented only after the program is running is both less reliable and guaranteed to limit the scope of the findings.

Traditional Evaluation Methods

As mentioned earlier, the goal of any new disability management programs may be the reduction of costs, increased employee satisfaction or, preferably, both. For most employers, however, the key internal selling point is cost reduction. But which costs are employers talking about? All too often employers look at figures that have been rolled up into a mysterious total without having an understanding of either what makes up that total or what the relationships are among program components, subtotals and the final program total. In addition, program totals almost never represent the true cost of disability. Indirect costs are generally ignored because savings in these areas are too difficult to measure or are perceived as somehow less important than the savings that come from direct cost figures. Yet, indirect costs are just as real as direct costs and should not be confused with so-called soft costs, which may be attributed to less tangible elements such as low morale and diminished quality of product or service.

Traditionally, the key success factors for disability management are reductions in lost workdays and the wage or salary replacement associated with them, medical charges and administration costs (e.g., budgets, vendor fees and premiums). Associated with these factors is a second tier of costs (see Exhibit 8A) that contributes to the first tier. Since most

COST RELATIONSHIPS

Success Factor (Reductions in . . .)	Second Tier Success Factor
Wage Replacement (including settlements and court decisions)	—Disability Duration —Litigation Rates and Costs —Modified/Light Duty RTW —Corporate Culture —Employee Satisfaction (with process and employment)
Medical Charges	—Disability Duration —Network Usage —Provider Utilization —Prescription Drug Utilization —Negotiated Charges
Administration Costs	—Vendor Pricing/Contract —Vendor Utilization —Experience Rating (Premium) —Process and Systems —Overhead —Salary and Benefits

employers track the costs in both tier one and two, the figures are generally used to compare the before and after effect of a new program. The problem with this approach is twofold. First, the scope is too limited. Focusing primarily on direct expenditures, employers miss the opportunity to measure costs and reap savings from indirect expenditures, productivity and employee satisfaction. Secondly, this method of comparison ignores the relationships that encompass cost drivers, environmental circumstances and program components. Thus, the employer may receive the *what* (cost savings), but with little or no knowledge of the *why* and *how* (relationship interaction). By leaving the why and how undefined, employers further miss the opportunity to maximize savings through redesign of the existing program or accurate targeting of additional programs/interventions.

Cause and Effect Evaluation Methods

Program evaluation follows a series of steps that mirror and interface with program development.

- ◆ Baseline assessment
- ◆ Modeling
- ◆ Implementation
- ◆ Management–program monitoring
- ◆ Outcomes assessment.

An employer can follow these steps regardless of the type of outcomes the evaluation is designed to measure. In the case of IDM, there are at least three types of outcomes that employers, consultants and service providers associate (to varying degrees) with such a program:

1. Costs (including productivity)[2]
2. Employee satisfaction
3. Market perception.

Costs and the productivity factor remain the primary focus for employers. However, there is an important growing trend to include employee satisfaction in the mix. Employers realize that employees need to be an active participant in the disability management process. As such, their perceptions of the process and of the employer in general may have an effect on such outcomes as incidence, duration, probability of litigation and, ultimately, the final cost of a claim. As a method of managing disability, the expectation for IDM is to increase employee satisfaction and thereby positively impact the outcomes mentioned. For instance, one of the major cost drivers in workers' compensation is litigation. Employees often run to lawyers because of perceptions built on the experience or beliefs of other employees, or due to a lack of understanding as to what to expect and where to find the necessary information to properly submit their claim and receive benefits. In the IDM model, the use of call center reporting and information lines provides the employee with the tools necessary to process their claim, while eliminating feelings of uncertainty and interceding on behalf of the employer to manage the misinformation received from other employees. This, in turn, reduces the need for an employee to seek lawyers to assist in the claim process, thereby reducing costs associated with litigation. See Exhibit 8B for elements that should be included in evaluation of employee satisfaction.

Market perception is an area that traditionally receives less attention than even employee satisfaction. Where it is touted more and more is in the area of benchmarking. Employers often use market perception/advantage as a blanket to protect themselves from sharing program sta-

Exhibit 8B

EVALUATING EMPLOYEE SATISFACTION

Contact Point With the Employee	Question Topics
Intake	• Ease of notification • Responsiveness of operator • Quality of benefit information provided • Quality of referral services • Open-ended comments
Claims Management	• Timeliness of initial follow-up • Responsiveness to questions • Timeliness of response to inquiries • Payment/benefit accuracy • Employer involvement • Open-ended comments
Medical Case Management	• Rapport with medical provider • Timeliness of initial follow-up • Responsiveness to questions • Timeliness of response to inquiries • Employer involvement • Open-ended comments
Return to Work	• Program type and effectiveness • Adjuster facilitation • Medical case manager facilitation • Employer facilitation • Medical provider facilitation • Co-worker perceptions • Open-ended comments
Denials	• Cause of denial • Quality of information provided regarding the appeals process • Responsiveness to questions • Perception of the appeals process (internal) • Open-ended comments

tistics with others in the industry. Other employers snidely smile at these excuses; they may have merit. Competition for good employees is growing, and an employer's ability to manage its benefit programs effectively relates to the types of benefits it can offer to entice a would-be candidate.

Therefore, while market perception may not have a direct bearing on the bottom line, there may be something to this outcome as it relates to employee recruitment, retention and ultimately to productivity.

Cost savings are the true selling point for implementing a disability program and remain the focal point for most employers. As such, the remainder of this chapter focuses primarily on evaluating programs from a cost perspective; however, employers are challenged to think about employee satisfaction and market perceptions as they design a program evaluation model.

Baseline Assessment

As part of the design phase of program development, the baseline assessment serves as the starting point for the measurement of program effectiveness and efficiency. Often referred to as a *total cost of disability or lost time study,* the process is similar to detective work. Most companies have only a vague idea as to what the true cost of lost time associated with disability is and how they should calculate it. Therefore, a total cost of disability study becomes part sorting through available figures and part estimating what is not currently captured. At its most basic level, the formula for the true cost of disability is

Direct Costs + Indirect Costs = Total Cost

Direct costs usually refer to three categories of benefit administration:
1. Paid-to-date benefits
2. Reserved benefits
3. Vendor fees and overhead costs.

Indirect costs are far more elusive. Often they embed themselves in other administration costs, become estimates using industry standards or are left uncalculated. Exhibit 8C identifies some of the broad buckets for both direct and indirect costs.

Indirect costs are often of greater importance to employers than they realize. For a large employer, the indirect costs of disability can be both staggering and eye-opening. Productivity alone can be the driver of costs equal to over 2.5% of payroll.[3] With the potential of so many lost dollars due to indirect costs of disability, why don't employers and vendors measure these costs accurately? The answer: There is little standardization in collecting, calculating and evaluating the information when available. Availability of information, in and of itself, is a problem for most employers and service providers. Experience with IDM has shown employers can do an adequate job of estimating costs for workers' compensation and long-term disability but have no ability to accurately track and measure

Exhibit 8C

COSTS OF DISABILITY

Direct Costs	Indirect Costs
Wage Replacement	Lost Productivity
Medical Costs	Overtime
Wage Reserves	Temporary Workers
Medical Reserves	Turnover
Administrative Overhead	Training
Insurance Premiums	Lost Time Due to Plan Waiting Periods
Vendor Fees	Short-Term Casual Absence
Legal Expenses	Safety Programs
Other Allocated Expenses	Employee Assistance Programs

costs associated with either short-term disability or casual absence. The first corrective step is to identify what needs to be captured and what can be estimated. Using the indirect cost buckets found in Exhibit 8C, Exhibit 8D identifies some basic methods for estimating indirect costs. Employers can use these methods as a model they can apply to additional indirect costs that are pertinent to their experience.

Once employers identify, estimate or calculate the direct and indirect costs, a snapshot of the current state becomes available. These figures provide the basis for before and after comparisons and support decisions regarding the type, location and timing of program interventions.

Modeling

If we think of the baseline assessment as the foundation of program evaluation, modeling is the structural framework built atop that foundation.

Modeling tells the story of the relationships between program components and desired outcomes. At this stage, the story has little substance, since it is based on theory rather than data. Nonetheless, the theoretical framework modeling provides is necessary to properly interpret the results of the evaluation. Without such a framework, the data becomes nothing more than a pile of descriptive statistics that can easily misrepresent the effectiveness or ineffectiveness of a program.

There are four steps to modeling, each one necessary to accurately

Exhibit 8D

METHODS FOR ESTIMATING INDIRECT COST

Indirect Cost	Method
Productivity	1. Output estimation[1] 2. Total wage loss—sum of the disabled workers wages, overtime wages allocated to cover for the absence and temporary help fees allocated to cover for the absence.
Overtime	1. Lower-bound estimate (proportional estimate)—total number of lost time hours divided by the total number of hours available for working, multiplied by the total number of overtime hours 2. Upper-bound estimate—total number of lost time hours divided by two[2] 3. Midpoint estimate—midpoint between the lower- and upper-bound estimates
Temporary Workers	1. Free estimate—total fee paid to the temporary employee agency 2. Employee wage loss—benefit replacement 3. Productivity factor—after calculating an average productivity factor, the factor is reduced by an estimate that takes into consideration the level of experience and expertise of a temporary worker 4. Fee + reduced productivity factor—the sum of the fee paid for a temporary worker and the difference between the average workers' productivity level and the reduced productivity of a temporary worker
Turnover	Probability of turnover for claimants multiplied by the average cost of worker replacement
Training	Component of worker replacement based on total cost of training programs divided by the average number of new employees (should be used as part of the turnover cost estimate; used a standalone cost estimate when the turnover cost estimate is not available)
Lost Time Due to Plan Waiting Periods	Total absence costs associated with casual absences managed under the group health plan or other supplemental plan during the waiting period for short-term disability or workers' compensation. These claims usually have duration that stays within the waiting period but have long-ranging effects on future health and absence issues.
Short-Term Casual Absence	One- to three-day absences with a cause, injury type or diagnosis that has the potential for becoming a short-term disability or workers' compensation claim
Safety Programs[3]	Total program costs
Employee Assistance Programs[4]	Total program costs

1. There are a variety of sources on measuring productivity within manufacturing industries. The best source to start with is the professional association for a given industry. For measuring white-collar/service sector output, see *Measuring White Collar Work* produced by the American Productivity and Quality Center of Houston, Texas.

2. This figure should be used as an upper bound only and must not exceed the total number of overtime hours worked.

3. Safety and EAP programs are more than just components of indirect costs. There are a number of direct and indirect costs associated with both programs that go beyond the scope of this chapter. As part of a total cost of disability study, the costs for these programs usually reflect budget allocations.

4. See note 3.

portray the expected relationships between program components and outcomes. These four steps include:

1. Articulating program interventions
2. Defining outcomes
3. Identifying the relationship between specific intervention and outcomes
4. Choosing a sampling method.

Articulating Program Interventions

Each intervention, or program component, needs to articulate the method of delivery. For instance, claims management has a number of components: claim intake, early intervention, investigation, telephonic case management and on-site case management, to name a few. Each of these components has an effect, either positive or negative, on the outcome of the claim (e.g., severity, duration and cost). In order to put each component (intervention) into a framework that links it with an outcome, parameters must be placed on the duration, measurement and scope of the intervention. *Duration* refers to the length of the episode as it relates to both absence and accruing expenses (e.g., medical bills). *Measurement* refers to the scale and data sources that are to be used for the modeling process. There are two primary scales for an intervention: dollar amount allocated and yes/no indicators that the intervention has occurred. Lastly, the *scope* of the intervention refers to the claim types, individuals, departments or other areas the intervention targets. In the case of claims management, some interventions apply to only certain subgroups of claims. Often the intervention is too costly to implement across all claim types. For example, to apply on-site case management to workers' compensation medical-only claims would likely have a negative effect on the total cost of the claim. Instead, on-site case management focuses on severe claims that characteristically have lost time, longer durations and a history of mismanagement on the part of medical providers.

Defining Outcomes

Following articulation of program interventions, employers need to define program outcomes. Employer goals generally drive a program and, therefore, dictate much of the design. However, goals by themselves can be vague and of little use in the evaluation process. To become useful, an operational definition must apply to each goal. The process of defining an outcome in operational terms has changed little since Shortell and Richardson outlined their techniques[4] to ensure both accuracy and consistent application of definitions throughout the evaluation process. Key guidelines to their technique include:

- ◆ Choose strong verbs that clearly indicate the result.
- ◆ State only one purpose per objective.
- ◆ Specify a single end product (result).
- ◆ Specify a time frame for achievement.

Identifying the Relationship Between
Specific Interventions and Outcomes

The essence of linking an intervention to an outcome is the issue of causality. Causality encompasses both direct and indirect effects. *Direct effects* refer to those relationships between intervention and outcome that can be depicted in a one-step process such as "A causes B." In contrast, *indirect effects* reflect a multistep process in the causal relationship such as "A causes C, which causes B." A third relationship about which evaluators need to be aware is called *spuriousness*. This type of relationship can put the results of an evaluation in jeopardy by misleading the evaluator in potentially both the design of the evaluation and the interpretation of the results. This relationship occurs when two variables (A and B) are believed to have a causal relationship (based on observation, logic or correlation statistics) but in reality the relationship is due to a third variable (C) that has a separate causal relationship with both A and B (C causes A and C causes B with no relationship between A and B). It is often difficult to predetermine spurious relationships. Therefore, it is essential for employers to pre-assess their models and identify places where an intervening cause could explain observed or expected outcomes. Once identified, employers need to develop alternative models and test both in the subsequent evaluation. While adding more development time, it guards against having to scrap an entire project due to poor modeling, or worse, the misinterpretation of results.

Once employers identify the key relationships, the next step is to develop the necessary statistical equations. The basis for analysis is the statistical method of linear regression. It is likely that linear regression will not meet all the needs of the evaluator due to data quality, interaction effects and/or sampling methods used. Similar to the description of the baseline assessment as the foundation for the evaluation process, linear regression serves as the foundation for the statistical adjustments that may be needed due to the circumstances mentioned and, for this reason, it is the method discussed in this chapter.

In brief, *regression analysis* is a statistical technique for modeling the relationship between population or process characteristics and outcomes.[5] The relationships between process characteristics and outcomes refers to both the relationship prior to and following the introduction of an intervention (or series of interventions). For instance, the lag time (an independent variable denoted as X_1) between the date of injury and when management of that injury begins is believed to have a relationship with the outcome of a claim in terms of duration and cost (a dependent variable denoted as $\hat{Y}_1$ and $\hat{Y}_2$, respectively). The use of this modeling technique allows the evaluator to:

◆ Determine the strength of relationships between independent and dependent variables and
◆ Operationalize the effect of independent variables on dependent variables.

Using this model to first measure the effect of the lag time on claim duration and/or cost, the evaluator can then add to the equation one or more independent variables that identify the program intervention(s) and measure its effect on the outcome. The resulting regression equation in mathematical term is:

$$\hat{Y}_n = a + b1X1 + b2X2 + ...bnXn$$

where $\hat{Y}_n$ represents either claim cost or duration (the dependent variable), a is a statistical constant based on the data, X_1 represents the lag time (independent variable 1), X_2 represents an intervention (independent variable 2), and X_n represents additional variables relating to the other interventions or control variables added to increase the accuracy of the measurement (independent variables 3... n). The variables b_1...n in the equation represent the variance in $\hat{Y}$ caused by a change in the corresponding X.

A hypothetical example: The average claims cost for Company ABC has been increasing over the last three years. In an effort to decrease the cost of their claims ($\hat{Y}$=claim cost), Company ABC initiates a study to identify the cost drivers for their claims. After collecting the data and running it through a regression model, Company ABC comes to the conclusion that one of their primary cost drivers is the lag time between the date of injury and when management of that injury begins (X_1=lag time). Based on their vendor's recommendation and market research into the effectiveness of telephonic, early intervention, Company ABC buys such a service from their current workers' compensation administrator. Using the cost allocated to each claim for telephonic, early intervention (X_2=allocated cost), the original cost model is altered to include this variable.

$$\hat{Y}_{claim\ cost} = a + b_1X_{lag\ time} + b_2X_{allocated\ cost} + ...b_nX_{control\ variables}$$

The model shows that while vendor fees have increased, the result of using telephonic, early intervention is saving $1.50 ($b_2$=1.5) for every

$1.00 ($X_2=1.0$) spent on the program. The conclusion is that telephonic, early intervention is a cost-effective program.[6]

Choosing a Sampling Method

There are two primary sampling methods for testing the results of a program or specific intervention. Both methods provide a means for developing comparison groups (an *experimental group* that receives the program or specific intervention and a *control group* that *does not* receive the program or specific intervention) on which the evaluation will be based (see Outcomes Assessment section). The differences between these two methods center on the selection process for each group.

The first method, randomized experimental design, is the preferred method from a scientific perspective. The results from this testing method are more valid, reliable and translatable. The use of randomized sampling guarantees that any member of the population studied has the same chance (probability) of being chosen for participation in either an experimental or control group. The element of randomization allows an evaluator to identify differences between groups associated with the implementation of the intervention and extrapolate those differences to the population from which these samples were drawn.

The second method, the site-matching, comparison group design, uses the judgment of the evaluator to create comparison groups based on a series of group characteristics. In the world of claims administration, the most logical matches begin at the unit or office level. For an employer, the starting point is likely to be at the facility level; however, some employers may find comparison groups based on division or department levels more appropriate. Exhibit 8E lists some of the characteristics (from both the employer and vendor perspective) that should be considered in the matching process.

Implementation

Implementation, from the perspective of the evaluation process, focuses on data collection. There are three primary sources of data:
1. One-on-one interviews
2. Surveys
3. Records.

Methods for collecting data will vary based on the type of information desired. One-on-one interviews generally collect qualitative data that aims at understanding a process as it is actually carried out on a daily basis. In many organizations, policies and procedures are often ignored or cir-

Exhibit 8E

COMPARISON CHARACTERISTICS

Common Characteristics	Employer Characteristics	Vendor Characteristics
• Staff size	• Job classification	• Client size
• Jurisdiction	• Job function	• Client industry (SIC code)
• Plan design	• Job title	• Revenue
• Administration design	• Employee income	• Fee structure/level
• Union involvement	• Department/division	
• Employee base/ demographics	characteristics	

cumvented. Identifying the reasons behind such behavior is often difficult and requires an intimate knowledge of both the policies and procedures, and the obstacles and challenges created by their implementation. One-on-one interviews (possibly supplemented with an audit) are the only method of data collection that provides the necessary detail to evaluate the usefulness of a given policy or procedure.

Surveys generally measure perceptions, such as the quality of service claimants experience. Surveys sit at the midpoint of a continuum of detail for data collection techniques. One-on-one interviews provide the greatest detail but are often time-consuming and expensive to implement. Surveys provide less detail but compensate the evaluator through their:

◆ Breadth of information
◆ Number of respondents reached
◆ Lower cost.

In the evaluation of an IDM program, surveys most often measure the satisfaction of employees with their claim-filing experience. This is a key element to the evaluation process as claimant satisfaction is often one of the goals outlined for an IDM program. IDM proponents argue that the integration process removes redundancies, provides a claimant with a single or at least fewer points of contact and offers claimants easy access to benefit and claim status information. These aspects of the IDM process have the potential to not only increase employee satisfaction, but thereby produce fewer litigated claims, lower turnover rates and shorter disability durations through better partnerships between the employer and the claimant. These outcomes, in turn, are directly associated with cost reductions both on a per claim and programwide basis.

Records are the most common form of data used when evaluating an IDM program. Records take a number of forms, but for advanced types of analysis the data elements themselves are used. The remaining two forms include the claim file (used for auditing) and third-party reports provided by vendors, other departments or outside analysis firms. The main issue with any form of data, but especially record data, is the quality of information. Data elements are only as useful as they are accurate. Dealing with miscoded and missing data is difficult and often becomes a silent force in the evaluation process. As the number of data elements miscoded or missing increases, the accuracy of the results will decrease unless a statistical method of adjustment is available. Because there is no flag that jumps out to say there are too many miscoded or missing data elements, the result is usually the misinterpretation of outcomes.

Miscoded classification of type, nature and cause for injuries is a rampant problem in the industry. It is not surprising to find anywhere from 25% to 50% of the data elements in these classifications unusable. However, employers and service providers are quick to use these figures to estimate patterns of incidence, develop program interventions and make other strategic decisions that impact both the risk experience of the company or client and eventually affect the bottom line. Simply put, "There is no substitute for accurate data."

Management–Program Monitoring

As stated previously, every program contains a series of components designed to produce specific outcomes. These outcomes represent the impact of both the component and the program. For instance, the use of clinical expertise during the management of a claim can potentially impact a number of issues such as provider visits, disability durations and the use of specialists. The effect of this component on outcomes is contingent upon a number of key implementation factors (such as timing, extent of use and tasks performed) that, when altered, may produce differences in outcomes. *Monitoring* tracks the delivery of these factors in order to determine the validity and reliability of outcomes and the need to alter implementation.

First, consider the concept of validity. *Validity* refers to the accuracy of the outcome. In other words, does the outcome answer the question? In claims management this may be more difficult to assess than under other circumstances. Researchers conducting a survey will often put in "check" questions designed to enhance or measure the validity of a response to more direct questions. Questions regarding fraudulent behavior serve as a good example. Asked if he or she has committed claimant fraud, a person may answer "no." However, the use of check questions about specific behaviors (e.g., taking more time off than is necessary or exaggerating an injury to obtain time off) may result in a very different interpretation of the individual's behavior. In this case, the direct response to the question regarding fraud becomes invalid as a result of the responses to the check questions.

In claims management, the concept is the same but the "check questions" are not always as obvious. This is due more to a lack of forethought than the ability to develop checks. As mentioned earlier, employers tend to jump the gun with development and implementation and forget the evaluation component. Desired outcomes need to be operationalized into measurable outcomes upfront as part of the design process. The desire to lower claim costs, for example, is too broad. Instead, what types of costs should employers measure: medical, indemnity, legal, overhead or training costs? How are they being affected? What else are these measures affecting and do they relate to costs? These are just a few of the questions that have to be asked during the design phase of program development.

Reliability refers to the consistency of the data. Within a claims database there are fields of information on every claim such as date of injury, date of birth, location where injury occurred, etc. In order for these fields to be reliable, an employer must standardize and monitor for compliance the data collection process. Different individuals entering the same data must produce the same results. This is one of the largest problems claims administrators face when trying to evaluate their program. Too often injuries are miscoded, dates are entered incorrectly or data is simply missing. For every piece of data that is miscoded or missing, that case has to be discarded, at least in part, when conducting an analysis. For some data elements, it is not uncommon that up to half of the cases have to be discarded for this reason. Such omissions and miscoding have a great effect on such common calculations as duration of disability, average cost per type of claim and incidence rates. Without such simple calculations, companies flounder in the dark as to what types of programs to implement and where or when to implement them.

Monitoring the ongoing implementation of a program adds to both the validity and reliability of the data gathered. Similar to the use of check questions and check data, monitoring serves as a check on the results of the impact assessment. This is accomplished by testing implementation with regard to whether program components are consistently applied and at what level of efficiency. Consistency in this context means two things:

1. The program reaches the population targeted (e.g., claimants, absentees, or claimants by injury types).
2. Program components are delivered without discrimination.

As part of the design phase, methods for collecting and checking data elements must be considered as part of larger quality assurance initiatives. The key is to balance what is realistic and cost effective with the level of validity and reliability desired. Generally, there are two methods used to monitor a program—audits and observation:

◆ Audits provide the employer a means to sample claim files for procedural compliance. By employing statistical methods of sampling, the employer can be fairly certain the results of the audit provide compliance trends for all claims filed. Thus, the employer can better assess the overall validity and reliability of program outcomes, as well as identify opportunities for enhancement.

◆ Observation is a technique usually employed by the claims handler. This method is less statistically sound but often provides more information (deeper understanding of compliance issues). In this technique, an observer watches one or two adjusters as they move through the adjusting process and asks questions when appropriate to clarify activities and the rationale for complying with and violating various procedures.

By far, the best option is to combine these two complementing methods. Audits should be conducted on an annual basis followed by the observation study. The number of claims audited will vary with the size of the employer; 100 usually suffices. As few as 30 can be used, but there are greater weaknesses in the ability to generalize from the findings.

Outcomes Assessment

While monitoring evaluates the implementation of program components, an outcomes assessment looks at the impact each component has on its target (e.g., cost, claimant behavior, disability duration and rate of litigation). Measuring impact, or effect, is calculated using one of two models. The first model assumes that we have all of the same information for the period before implementation that we have for the period after implementation. This model uses a Pre-Post Case Comparison design.[7] The effect of the program is the change in the outcome variable from the preimplementation period to the postimplementation period at the treatment site minus the change in the outcome variable from the preimplementation period to the postimplementation period at the comparison site. The idea is by subtracting the change at the comparison site, we control for any other factors extraneous to the reform effort that might have an effect on outcomes over the period. In mathematical terms, the model is:

Effect = (Posttreatment−Pretreatment)−(Postcomparison−Precomparison)

While this model is always preferable when information is available for both the postimplementation and the preimplementation periods, there may be cases in which the information is unknown. In situations where pretreatment and precomparison data is not available, differences between the treatment and comparison sites in the postimplementation period are used as follows:

Effect = Posttreatment−Postcomparison

It is the difference between these two models that illustrates the need for inclusion of the evaluation process in the design and implementation phases of a program. During the design phase, employers need to be developing a means of calculating a baseline for their current program. This includes both cost and cost-related (e.g., employee satisfaction) data. Without such data, employers limit themselves to the posttreatment/postcomparison model. Inevitably, if a new program is designed to enhance data collection capabilities there will be areas that have to be assessed using the postimplementation model, but standard data elements such as indemnity payments, medical payments and reserves should not be ignored because they are likely to show the largest impact.

Summary

The evaluation process must mirror the program. It should be developed concurrently with the program to be evaluated. To wait until after program development has begun, or the program has been implemented, will at best provide a skewed picture of program effectiveness and, at worse, prevent the evaluation altogether.

The process of evaluation begins and ends with data. The baseline assessment provides the starting point from which both program design and evaluation begins. Based on the goals of a program and its design, the evaluation process moves to modeling relationships through:

◆ Articulation of program interventions
◆ Definition of program outcomes
◆ Connecting specific interventions with specific outcomes
◆ Choosing a testing method.

Implementation of the program is concurrent with the implementation of the evaluation model. Using primarily record sources of data (data elements), the collection process transcends the management phase of the process as implementation of both the program and the evaluation model are monitored to ensure valid and reliable outcomes. Those outcomes are then assessed and conclusions are drawn as to both the effectiveness and efficiency of the program.

Endnotes

1. With the investment in time and resources so high, employers are often intimidated by the concept of IDM. However, the real source of their fears stems from a lack of data on the one hand and the inability to effectively use data to evaluate the cost benefit of a program on the other. As the IDM concept continues to evolve, advancements in intake processes and software applications are providing employers with more consistent and accurate data that forms the basis for the cost/benefit analysis.

2. Productivity is often thought of as an indirect cost, which is the definition used in this chapter. A second approach is to define productivity in terms of revenue instead of as an expenditure. Both methods are equally valid and the use of the term *usually* depends on the evaluator's or employer's orientation.

3. 1996 unpublished total cost of disability study conducted by IntegraComp LLC.

4. Stephen M. Shortell and William C. Richardson, *Health Program Evaluation,* St. Louis: C.V. Mosby, 1978.

5. This discussion of regression analysis is designed to familiarize the reader with some of the basic concepts and interpretations that are possible with using this modeling technique. It is not designed to be a comprehensive treatise on how to conduct regression analysis or to identify the strengths, weaknesses and statistical adjustments necessary to apply the model properly and interpret the results accurately. Readers interested in learning more about regression analysis and other modeling techniques should contact a claims administrator, a consultant that provides evaluation services or a statistician.

6. This model assumes a normal distribution with a mean of 0 and a standard deviation of 1.

7. The source of information on the Pre-Post Case Comparison design is Jonathan Crane, Director of the National Center for Research on Social Programs.

Section IV

Additional Resources

Organizations

Integrated Benefits Institute, a nonprofit research, benchmarking and information organization

Thomas Parry, President
William Molmen, General Counsel
Integrated Benefits Institute
525 Market Street, Suite 740
San Francisco, CA 94105
Phone: (415)222-7280
Fax: (415)222-7281
E-mail: ibi@ibiweb.org
www.ibiweb.org

Disability Management Employer Coalition (DMEC)

DMEC, a not-for-profit organization founded in 1992 to advance the development of integrated disability management processes in al! disability-related employer programs

Sharon Kaleta, Chairman
Phone: (619)468-3481
E-mail: chairman@dmec.org
Marcia Carruthers, Executive Director
Phone: (619)780-0066
E-mail: exec.dir@dmec.org
Wendy Yale, Administrative Director
Phone: (800)789-3632
Disability Management Employer Coalition
5694 Mission Center Road, #310
San Diego, CA 92108-4328
www.dmec.org

Case Studies

While equally pertinent to employers considering or implementing an IDM program, the two case studies that follow stress different concerns. Case Study A links organizational climate to impact on accidents and disability. Case Study B evaluates a specific integrated service and its effect on claim duration, cost and administration.

Notes

Case Study A stems from research presented in "Organizational Climate and Ineffectiveness: Evidence from 25 Outdoor Work Crew Divisions," co-authored by Edward L. Anderson, Adam Stetzer and Frederick P. Morgeson and reported in the *Journal of Quality Management*, 2 (1997).

Case Study B was prepared by CIGNA IntegratedCare in July 1998.

Case Study A: Organizational Climate and Its Impact on Accidents and Disability

The Objective

To determine the impact an organization's climate has on accidents and disability, several variables related to the Total Quality Management approach and representative of high performance work climates were investigated:

- ◆ Quality—the extent to which an organization fosters the pursuit of quality goals
- ◆ Cooperation—the extent to which individuals and groups within an organization can work together
- ◆ Customer service—the extent to which an organization is oriented to the customer
- ◆ Overall climate—the extent to which the above variables combine to produce a high performance work climate.

These variables were then linked to objective measures of organizational ineffectiveness (i.e., numbers of accidents and absences).

Hypothesis

Organizations that have positive quality, cooperation and customer service climates are likely to experience fewer accidents and absences.

Study Methodology

Population Sample

The population studied was 14,553 nonexempt employees, all on outdoor work crews, from 25 divisions of a large utility company. All the divisions had similar structures, work processes and technology. Each division was highly autonomous, however, and likely to have its own unique climate and policies.

Data Collection

Organizational climate data was collected via a confidential survey–with a response rate of 45%–measuring employee attitudes regarding quality, cooperation and customer service. (The responses were validated as being reliable in measuring the attributes assessed.) Organizational ineffectiveness data on number of accidents (recordable incidents per Occupational Safety and Health Administration standards) and on number of absences of 8-14 days' duration was also collected. This absence duration was selected because:

- The company only kept records on short-term disability (STD) benefit-related absences. (STD kicks in after seven consecutive days of disability.)
- The company considered any absence lasting more than 14 days to be serious and nondiscretionary.

Study Results

Results, adjusted for age, tenure and division size as control variables, were as follows:

- Higher average ratings of quality climate were associated with lower accident and absence rates.
- More cooperative climates were associated with lower accident and absence rates.
- An overall high performance work climate was associated with lower accident and absence rates.
- A climate of customer service was not significantly related to accident or absence rates.

Discussion

- The literature has shown that quality climates produce improved productivity and revenue.
- The research demonstrates a link between quality climates and organizational ineffectiveness, such that positive climates were associated with lower accident and absence rates. (This is important because lost health-related productivity is a nonconformance measurement of a corporation's human capital.)
- Efforts focused on creating quality climates reduce ineffectiveness without the tradeoffs (such as decreased safety) that might be expected.

Case Study B: Preliminary Performance Analysis of CIGNA Integrated Care's *Ability* Returns^{sm} for Employer A

Executive Summary

Employer A implemented CIGNA Integrated Care's *Ability*Returns product to help manage disability and workers' compensation benefits and reduce associated costs. This analysis uses a matched sample methodology to compare various measures of the disability program before and after *Ability*Returns. The study provides preliminary information based on available experience (as of July 1998).

Key Findings

- ◆ Integrated telephonic intake reduced average claim reporting time by 35-54%.
- ◆ Effective care/claim management reduced STD durations by 15-20%.
- ◆ STD claim costs decreased proportionately.

These findings indicate that *Ability*Returns is effective in reducing duration and cost of short-term disability claims. These reductions are based on actual claims experience and persist after age, gender and diagnosis adjustments, indicating genuine program impact. Telephonic intake increases the efficiency and timeliness of the process and provides better service to the employees.

The accompanying analysis describes the preliminary findings in greater detail and describes the methodologies used in the study. At the present time, there is an insufficient volume of closed long-term disability or workers' compensation claims to determine program impact in these areas. This is, in part, due to the longer average duration of these types of claims and the short analysis period. As sample sizes increase, further studies will be conducted.

Introduction

Employer A has implemented CIGNA's *Ability*Returns product as part of its developing integrated benefits program. *Ability*Returns provides integrated workers' compensation and disability management services to the company's employees. These services are designed to reduce the costs and duration of occupational and nonoccupational disability and, thus, help *Employer A* minimize benefit costs, maximize productivity and grow its market position.

Employer A is a holding company providing policy and management direction and support for three companies: Subsidiary I, Subsidiary II and Subsidiary III. In 1997, these subsidiary companies employed over 7,500 employees.

The company has a long history of innovation and community involvement. Its most important assets are its people, who help the company sustain its market position with the help of modern technology and business processes. *Ability*Returns is a key part of *Employer A's* progressive business strategy.

*Ability*Returns provides the following services:
- ♦ A single toll-free telephone number to report occupational and nonoccupational disabilities
- ♦ Clinically based claims review and assignment
- ♦ Nurse-based care management with extensive use of clinical and duration guidelines
- ♦ Effective claims administration
- ♦ Appropriate use of vocational rehabilitation.

These services are designed to accomplish the following:
- ♦ Reduce claims duration and cost
- ♦ Facilitate timely claims reporting and assessment
- ♦ Simplify claims administration.

This analysis is intended to provide preliminary information on the performance of *Ability*Returns for *Employer A* based on experience to date. This initial study is limited to short-term disability claims experience. There is an insufficient volume of long-term disability and lost-time workers' compensation claims to support credible analysis at this time.

Study Design

The study was designed to provide initial feedback on the performance of *Ability*Returns based on the experience to date. Since less than 10% of *Employer A's* employees have been in *Ability*Returns for more than six months, the scope of this study is limited.

Employer A implemented *Ability*Returns in four distinct groups:

Group	Employees	Effective Date
Location 1	~ 445	01/01/97
Location 2	~ 800	11/15/97
Location 3	~ 240	12/01/97
All Other Employees	~ 5,460	01/01/98

A matched sample design was used to provide for accurate pre/postprogram comparisons. This approach creates groups of claims that have been incurred and closed within the same time parameters to allow for appropriate comparison without bias due to differences in the development periods.

Phases of Study

For the purposes of this analysis, the experience was divided into two phases. Phase 1 represents Location 1, a small number of employees with an incurred year of experience before and with the *Ability*Returns program. Phase 2 represents all other locations, a large number of employees over a shorter four-month incurred period, with comparable preprogram periods. The groups for each phase were set up as follows:

Phase 1

- ◆ Pregroup: All Location 1 claims incurred in 1996 and closed by 4/30/97.
- ◆ Postgroup: All Location 1 claims incurred in 1997 and closed by 4/30/98.

These groups contain a subset of claims that have matched incurred and development periods. The results are directly comparable between groups, but do not reflect the final performance of all claims incurred within each period, since some claims from October and November of each incurred year could still have been open in this sample. As such, the actual duration and claim cost for fully developed closed claims incurred during each year will be nominally higher than reported here.

Phase 2

- ◆ Pregroup 95: All non-Location 1 claims incurred and closed 1/1/95–4/30/95.
- ◆ Pregroup 96: All non-Location 1 claims incurred and closed 1/1/96–4/30/96.
- ◆ Pregroup 97: All non-Location 1 claims incurred and closed 1/1/97–4/30/97.
- ◆ Pregroup 98: All non-Location 2 claims incurred and closed 1/1/98–4/30/98.

These groups contain a subset of claims that have matched incurred and development periods. The results are directly comparable to assess program impact, but represent only a portion of the claims that were incurred in each period. The duration and cost measures of all claims incurred during these matched quarters will increase as the claims develop and close. This sample is reviewing only those claims that opened and closed with the analysis period.

The first four months of each year were selected so consistent comparisons could be made over a number of previous time periods. Subsequent analyses will require some adjustment of these analytical groups to account for the slightly different implementation dates (11/15/97 for Location 2, 12/1/97 for Location 3 and 1/1/98 for the rest). These adjustments were not made at this time because they would result in sample sizes that were too small to analyze. The analysis period selected for this phase is common across each of the included locations.

The matched design affords two independent assessments of *Ability-Returns* performance for *Employer A*. The first reflects how the program has performed for the Location 1 plant for an entire year. The second compares performance for the remainder of the company during the first four months, compared with equivalent periods for the previous three years. Taken together, these independent views help determine the presence and magnitude of program impact.

Measurements

The study analyzed several key measurements including:
- ◆ Average Disability Duration: The average number of days between

the date the illness or injury was incurred and the date the claim was closed. It reflects calendar days.

◆ Average Claim Cost: The average total amount paid on the claim for the benefit duration.

◆ Average Reporting Time: The average number of days between the date the illness or injury was incurred and the date the claim was reported. It reflects calendar days.

◆ Claim Incidence Rate: The number of claims per 100 covered employees.

The analysis compared these key metrics across pre/postgroups. In addition, the data for each phase was adjusted by age, gender and diagnosis to control for potential differences between the "mix" of claims in each group.

Age, gender and diagnosis adjustment is basically a two-step process. The first step is to subset each group for claims with common age groups, gender and diagnoses. The second step is to reweigh or distribute the average durations of the postgroup to the distribution of the pregroup. This makes each group directly comparable. Resulting differences in benefit duration observed are then due directly to the program impact. The influence of differences in age, gender and diagnoses are effectively removed.

Key Findings and Discussion

Claim Reporting Time

Telephonic intake reduced the time to report short-term disability claims to CIGNA by 35-50% depending on the phase and group. *Claim reporting time* is defined as the number of days between the date an illness or injury was incurred and the date the claim was reported to CIGNA.

Before *Ability*Returns, claims were reported using a combination of mail, fax and telephone. The process involved completion of a variety of paperwork. With *Ability*Returns, claims are reported telephonically through a single toll-free telephone number. This affords more timely and accurate claims processing. (See Figure 1.)

The average time to report a claim in the Location 1 plant was 12.8 days prior to *Ability*Returns, and 8.3 days with *Ability*Returns. This represents a 35% reduction in the time to report a claim. Using telephonic intake, the average claim is now being reported just around the time the waiting period is ending, rather than the point at which the first check was expected. Similar findings were observed for the Phase 2 group covering the rest of the company. (See Figure 2.)

In this situation, there was a mild decline in the pre-*Ability*Returns

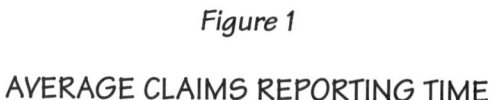

Figure 1

AVERAGE CLAIMS REPORTING TIME

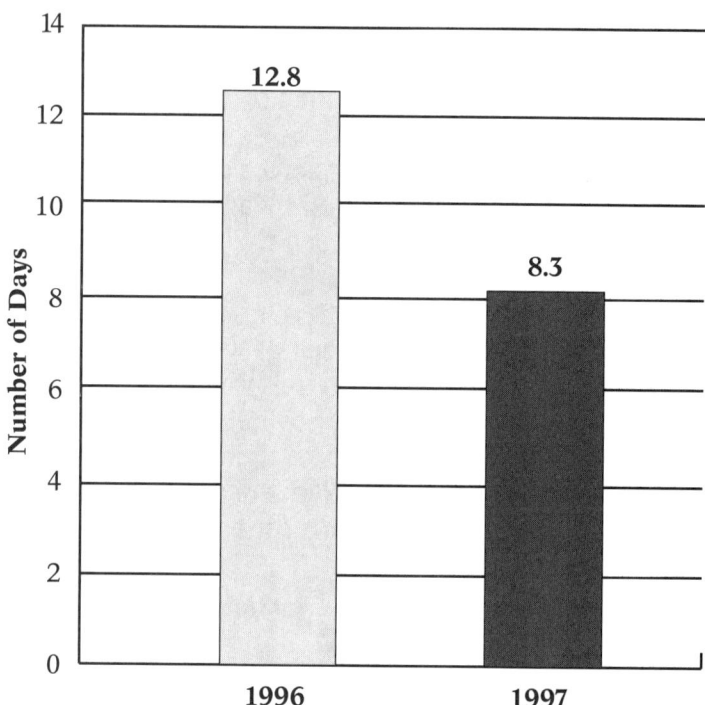

reporting time based on *Employer A's* history, with a significant change with the onset of *Ability*Returns. The "Other Clients" bars in Figure 2 reflect average claim reporting time for familiar policies for CIGNA's other clients. *Employer A's* historical reporting has been faster than CIGNA's book of business for similar disability contracts. The decrease due to *Ability*Returns is much greater than that of the book of business for the same time. CIGNA's book of business reporting times are decreasing due to incremental installation of telephonic reporting for its clients. The changes in the reference figures reflect an increasing percentage of CIGNA's other clients using this newer technology.

The general reception of the telephonic claims process by employees and plant medical/human resources personnel has been very positive. As the program was initially implemented, there were some operational issues regarding who would report claims (employee or employer), and the process for reporting (before, during or after work).

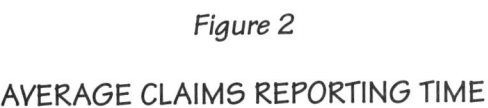

Figure 2

AVERAGE CLAIMS REPORTING TIME

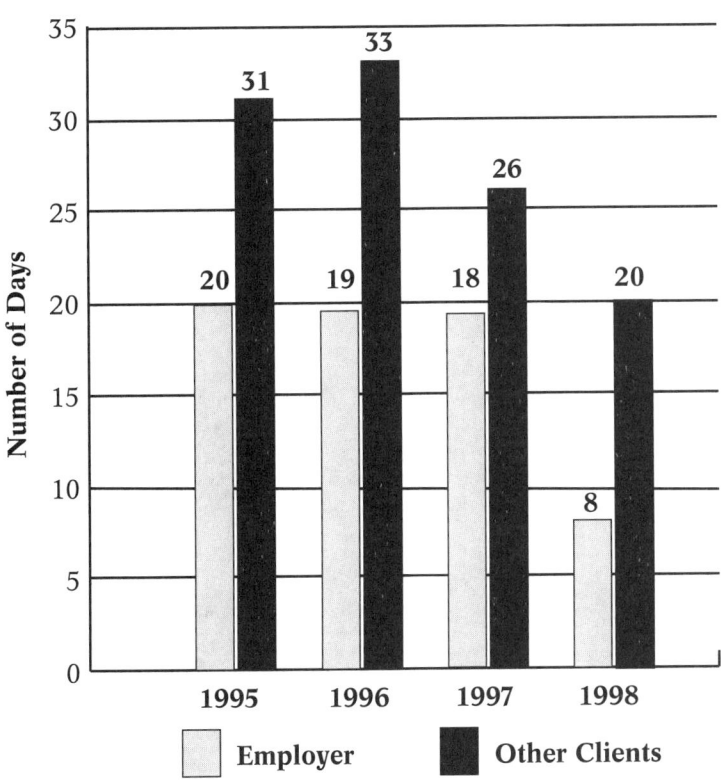

Working collaboratively with corporate benefits and CIGNA, *Employer A* developed standard processes to report claims. Occupational claims would be reported by the employer, while nonoccupational claims would be reported by the employee. The nurses developed procedures to report workers' compensation claims in a timely fashion rather than in batches so intakes can be handled efficiently, and reporting times are minimized. This team-oriented approach has contributed greatly to the reduction in reporting times. Consistent application of these processes will maintain and possibly reduce reporting times further.

Disability Duration

The average disability duration was reduced 15% in Phase 1 (Location 1) and 20% in Phase 2 (the rest of the company) groups.

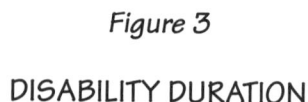

Figure 3

DISABILITY DURATION

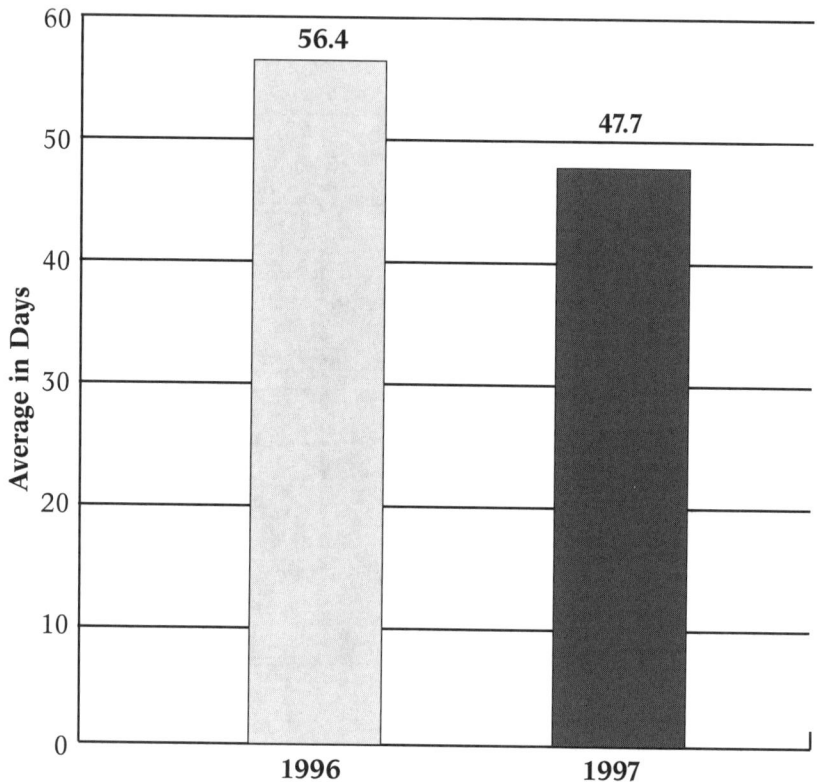

1996   1997

Phase 1 (Location 1): Phase 1 included all employees in Location 1. Claims incurred in 1996 and closed through 4/30/97 were considered part of the "pre" *Ability*Returns group. Claims incurred in 1997 and closed through 4/30/98 were part of the *Ability*Returns program.

*Ability*Returns claims in the Location 1 group have an average duration of 47.7 days, which is 15% less than the 56.4 days in the pre-program period. (See Figure 3.) Because the samples are matched for incurred and closed periods, the numbers are directly comparable.

Due to the sample "window," the claims in each group do not represent a complete picture of the location's experience. Claims that had not closed by April 30 of each year were not included in this study. If all claims for these incurred periods were included when they closed, the average durations will be somewhat higher, but the expected program impact will

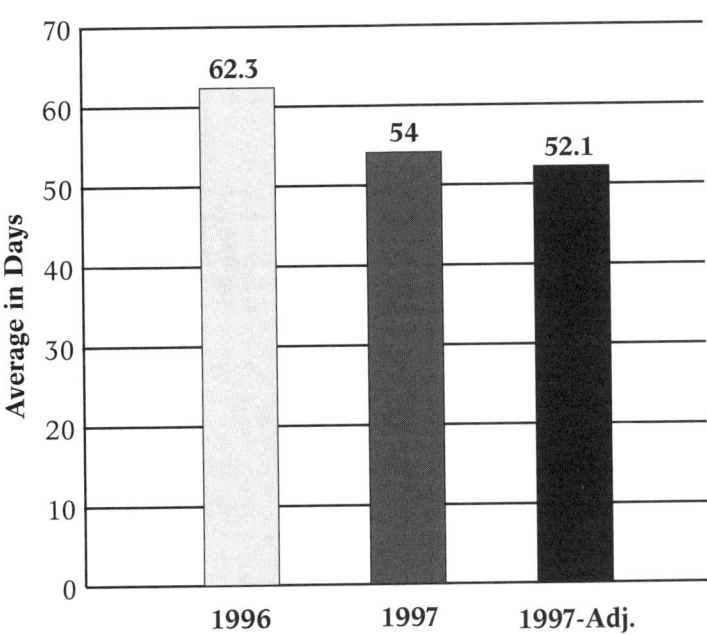

Figure 4

DISABILITY DURATION—ADJUSTED

remain. Therefore, subsequent analyses of the same time periods will show different durations for the same periods.

It is possible that differences in the mix of ages, genders and diagnoses between analytical periods could be responsible for some of the observed difference in benefit durations. To control for this possibility, the data was age-, gender- and diagnosis-adjusted. This statistical technique effectively normalizes the samples for variation in these three areas and provides a more accurate picture of program impact.

When the data is adjusted (see Figure 4), it is necessary to subset the pre- and postsample groups for claims with common age, gender and diagnoses. Since these groups are now a subset of their original samples, their unadjusted durations will vary from the results presented for the location overall. In this case, the average durations for the raw pre/postdata is higher for the adjustment subset (Figure 4) than for the total sample (Figure 3).

However, when the 1997 *Ability*Returns data is adjusted for the same age, gender and diagnosis distribution of the pre-*Ability*Returns experience, the shorter observed durations are preserved. This means the decreased duration observed during *Ability*Returns is not due to differences in age, gender or diagnostic mix.

For this sample, the age-, gender- and diagnosis-adjusted data indicates the *Ability*Returns claims had a 16% lower duration than the same types of claims had in the preprogram period. The adjusted duration on the subset of claims is of similar magnitude to the unadjusted changes on the complete sample.

Phase 2 (All locations except Location 1): Phase 2 includes all locations except the Location 1 plant. Since this group has only been using *Ability*Returns since 1/1/98, our program group can only include claims that were incurred and closed within the first four months of the year. To make valid comparisons, we created multiple sample groups for previous years. This allowed us to determine if the immediate pre-*Ability*-Returns period was representative of *Employer A's* previous history. Since the sample window includes claims that opened and closed within the first four months of each year, the average durations are logically lower than our Phase 1 group. As all of the claims from the incurred periods close, the average durations will increase.

The pre-*Ability*Returns periods for 1995, 1996 and 1997 had disability durations between 25.6-26.9 days. Contrast this with the 20.6-day duration for the claims experience in *Ability*Returns. (See Figure 5.)

*Ability*Returns claims in the Phase 2 group had an average duration of 20.6 days, which is 20% less than the 25.6-26.9 days in the preprogram period. These findings are of similar magnitude to those of the Phase 1 group, but are based on an independent sample. The presence of similar program effects in two independent views of the same client's experience increases the credibility of the findings. This also suggests that the impact of *Ability*Returns on STD durations is relatively consistent and could be predicted based on early-stage claims experience.

The darker bars in Figure 5 represent the average duration of other CIGNA STD clients with similar policy/contract structures. These figures were derived using the same sample construction process and are comparable to *Employer A's* experience. There is a slight, but progressive decrease in the average duration of the CIGNA book of business experience over time. This probably reflects industry trends that correspond to better medical care, coupled with ongoing improvements in claims management. During the pre-*Ability*Returns period, *Employer A* experienced a similar mild decline consistent with the overall book of business.

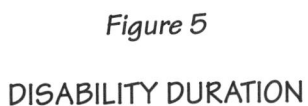

Figure 5

DISABILITY DURATION

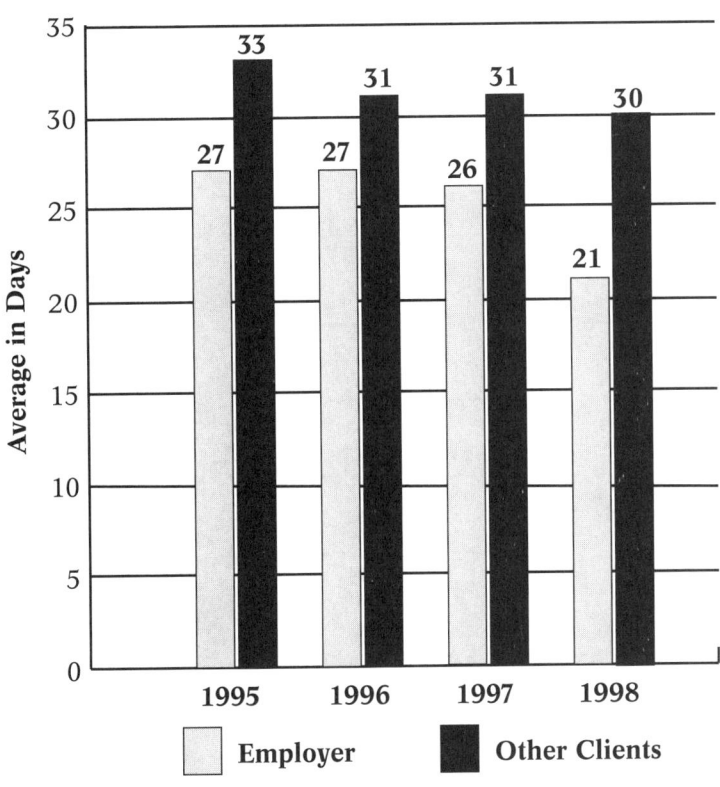

However, with *Ability*Returns, there was a significant decrease in duration, indicating significant incremental program effects.

As is the case with the Location 1 population, the positive *Ability*-Returns program impact continues after age, gender and diagnosis adjustment for the populations between the sample periods.

Both phases of *Employer A's Ability*Returns program show significant reductions in the duration of their STD claims. This difference is present in both the raw and age-, gender-, and diagnosis-adjusted data. (See Figure 6.)

Claim Cost

Average claim cost decreased significantly with *Ability*Returns. If the mix of employees with the same salaries and benefit types is consistent

Figure 6

DISABILITY DURATION—ADJUSTED

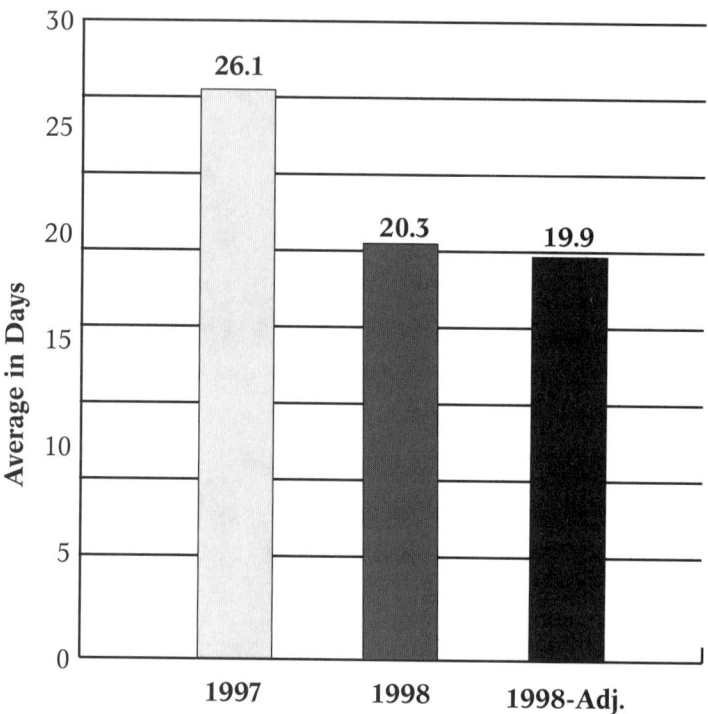

across analysis periods, then the average claim cost should decrease in similar proportion to decreased duration. *Employer A* has two basic STD plans—one for hourly employees and the other for salaried employees. The hourly plan pays a flat $125/week benefit. The salaried plan pays between 60% and 100% of wages for 13-26 weeks, depending on length of service or salary grade.

Average claim cost in this analysis reflects claims from both the hourly and salaried populations. As such, the effective decrease in claim cost will vary based on the mix of hourly and salaried employees.

Phase 1 (Location 1): For the Location 1 group, the average claim cost decreased 8% from $873/claim to $804/claim. (See Figure 7.) The fact that the claim cost decreased a bit less than the duration suggests that the *Ability*Returns group in 1997 included a greater percentage of salaried employees.

Phase 2 (All locations except Location 1): The remaining locations

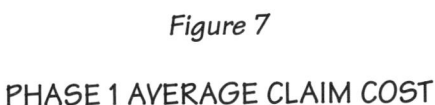

Figure 7

PHASE 1 AVERAGE CLAIM COST

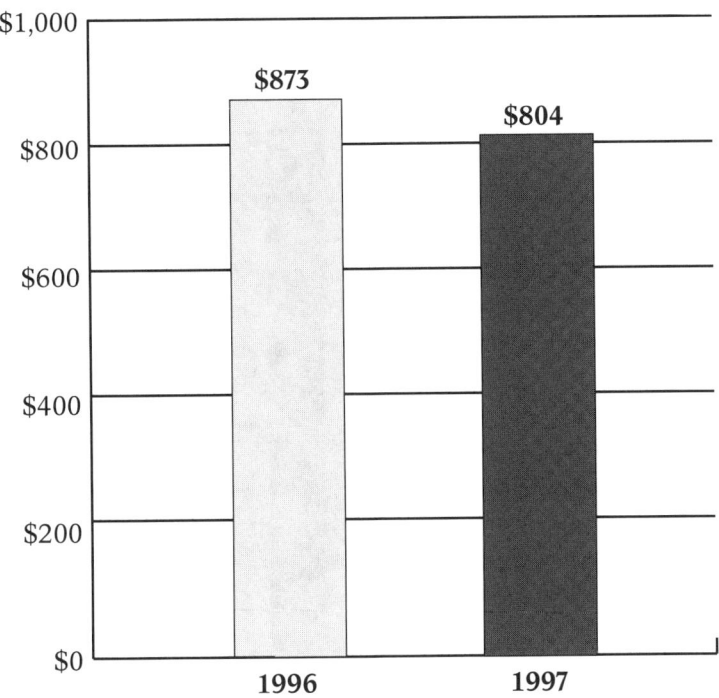

also experienced decreased claim costs coincident with the decreased durations. This group experienced a 24% decrease from $402 for the 1997 preprogram period to $304 for the program period. (See Figure 8.)

Both phases experienced a significant decrease in average claim cost due to *Ability*Returns. The magnitude of these changes reflects a mix of hourly and salaried employees and, therefore, does not directly correspond to the decrease in duration. (Note the actual values for the average cost per claim reflect the sample period and are lower than would be expected when all the incurred claims are closed.)

Claim Incidence

Total claim costs are a function of the number of claims and the du-

Figure 8

PHASE 2 AVERAGE CLAIM COST

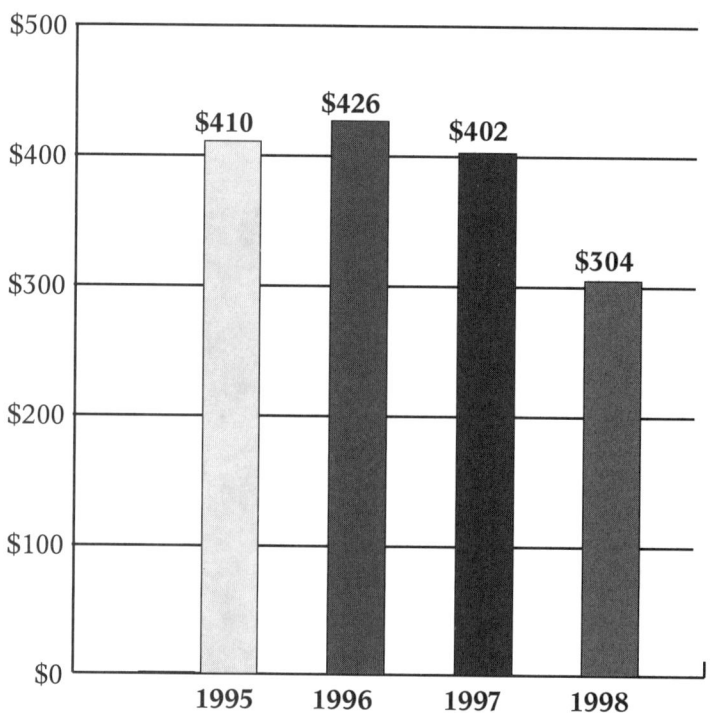

ration or unit cost of those claims. The number of claims during any period is generally a function of the number of covered employees, the stability of their employment and a number of issues surrounding seasonal influences. Up to this point, we have discussed the positive impact of *Ability*Returns on benefit duration, claim cost and claim reporting. This section will discuss trends influencing the number of claims experienced by *Employer A*.

Claims can be expected to vary as a function of the covered population. As such, it is often more useful to understand the incidence of claims as a function of the covered population.

Phase 1 (Location 1): At Location 1 the incidence of claims per 100 employees increased almost 37% over the previous year. (See Figure 9.)

Of the claims profiled, the number of nonpregnancy claims for females increased slightly, from 17 claims to 19 claims. The mix of these

Figure 9

PHASE 1 CLAIM INCIDENCE

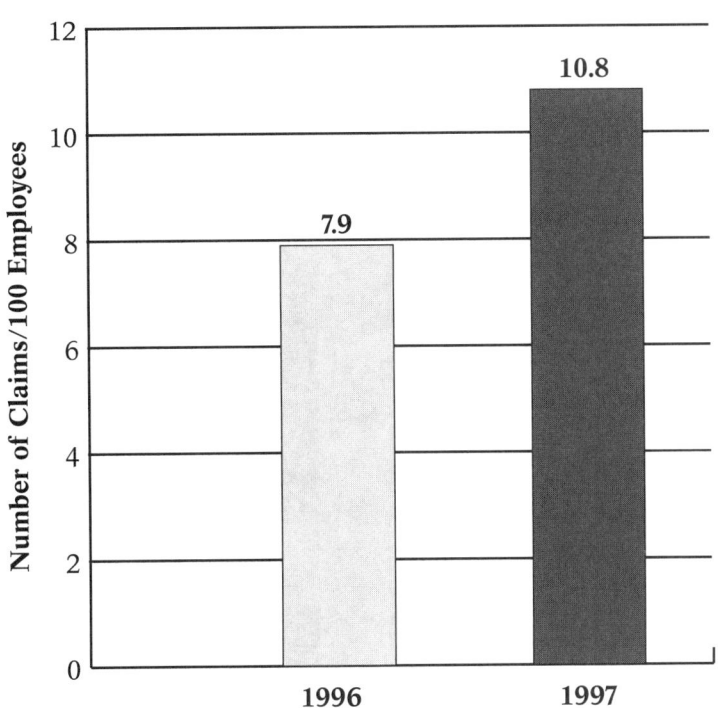

claims changed a bit. There was a decrease in the number of mental illness claims for females, but an increase in the number of digestive-related disorders, genitourinary and musculoskeletal problems. There is no pattern among these claims. Pregnancy claims increased 30% from 10 to 13 across the groups. It is interesting to note, however, that the number of disability claims filed by male employees increased 60% from 10 to 16 across these periods. All increases in male claims fell into the Accident-Injury category. Review of the injury types or affected body parts showed no pattern. The size of the Phase 1 group is small, and a broader range of variability is expected. The change in utilization in this group should be monitored.

Phase 2 (all locations except Location 1): The claims rate for the Phase 2 group remained virtually constant with previous periods. (See Figure 10.) The incidence rates were exposure adjusted to compensate for the short analysis period. The incidence rates are within the range of

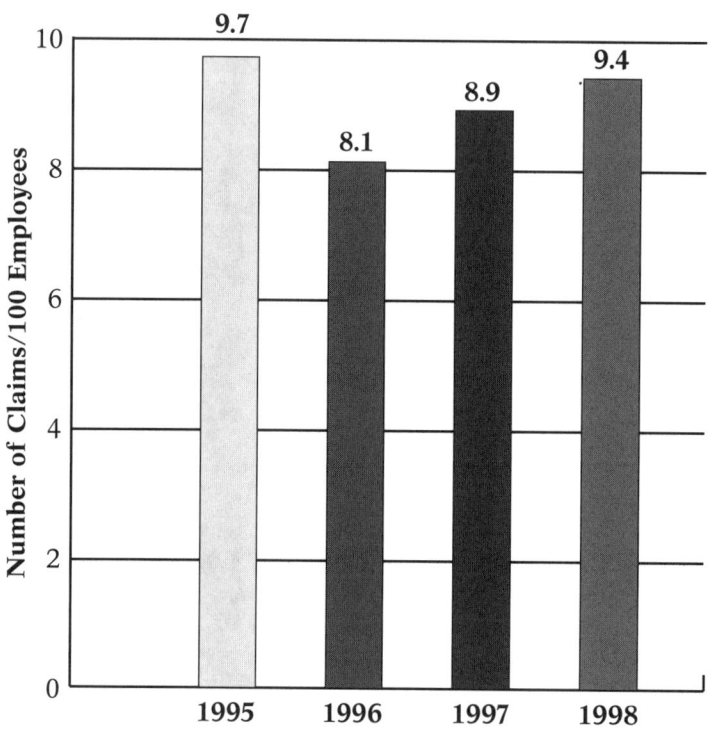

Figure 10

CLAIM INCIDENCE EXPOSURE—ADJUSTED

normal variability based on earlier time periods. The sample size for this population is much larger, so variability within the group is lower.

The absence of significant changes in the underlying incidence of claims indicates that *Employer A* will see the impact of decreased duration and claim costs achieved through *Ability*Returns. Review of incidence rates in aggregate will show a more stable pattern than when viewed at the plant or location level. This is to be expected due to the differences in sample sizes.

The similarity of the incidence rates under *Ability*Returns for the Location 1 population, and the pre/post rates for the rest of the company suggest actual incidence rates observed under *Ability*Returns are not unusually higher than the pervious year; rather, the previous year may have been unusually low. Incidence rates will continue to be monitored to see if there is an underlying trend.

Summary

This preliminary analysis reviews the performance of CIGNA Integrated Care's *Ability*Returns product of *Employer A*. *Employer A* implemented *Ability*Returns in four groups. The analysis was conducted in two phases, grouping similar locations based on the amount of experience in the program. The study uses a matched sample design to review short-term disability claims experience for each phase. Phase 1 (Location 1) covers claims incurred in 1996 (pre-*Ability*Returns) with claims incurred in 1997 (with *Ability*Returns). Only claims incurred within each year and closed by April of the following year were included so that the samples were comparable. Phase 2 (entire company less Location 1) covers claims incurred and closed within the first four months of each year. Claims in the sample periods for 1995, 1996 and 1997 were considered pre-*Ability*Returns, while claims incurred in 1998 were considered as part of the program group. At the present time, there is an inadequate volume of long-term disability or lost-time workers' compensation claims to conduct meaningful analysis.

The study found each study group (Phase 1 and Phase 2) had three very similar findings:

1. The time to report claims was reduced by 35-54% by using telephonic claim reporting and intake.
2. Short-term disability claim durations were reduced by 15-20%.
3. There were corresponding decreases in short-term disability claim costs.

The changes in claim duration persisted after statistical adjustment for differences in age, gender and diagnosis, substantiating the positive impact of *Ability*Returns.

Based on this preliminary data, it is clear *Ability*Returns has been successful in helping *Employer A* in the following areas:

- ◆ Improve claims reporting and processing
- ◆ Reduce claim durations
- ◆ Reduce claim costs.

As *Employer A's* experience with *Ability*Returns increases, additional studies incorporating analysis of program impact on other benefit areas will be conducted.

Case Study Appendix
EMPLOYEE DISTRIBUTION

Employer's employees can be divided into 11 key groups based on location or affiliation (e.g., corporate, location 3). Within each of these groups, employees are classified as either salaried or hourly. Of the company's 8,000 employees, approximately 7,000 are covered for benefits. The distribution of covered employees by group is summarized in the following table. This information was used to calculate claim incidence rates.

EMPLOYEE DISTRIBUTION[1]

Location	Employee Group	1995	1996	1997	1998 YTD[2]
Location 1	Hourly	450	431	407	393
	Salaried	41	40	38	33
	Total	491	471	445	426
Location 2A	Hourly	528	475	502	512
	Salaried	60	60	55	50
	Total	588	535	557	562
Location 4	Hourly	793	741	755	735
	Salaried	125	131	127	126
	Total	918	872	882	861
Location 5	Hourly	375	380	321	333
	Salaried	28	29	29	27
	Total	403	409	350	360
Location 6	Hourly	0[3]	1182	898	823
	Salaried	196	120	89	84
	Total	196	1302	987	907
Location 7	Hourly	1276	1270	1146	1097
	Salaried	178	190	200	192
	Total	1454	1460	1346	1289

EMPLOYEE DISTRIBUTION (Continued)

Location	Employee Group	1995	1996	1997	1998 YTD
Location 2B	Hourly	237	247	223	196
	Salaried	19	18	17	17
	Total	256	265	240	213
Location 8	Hourly	1580	1496	1403	1458
	Salaried	106	106	101	100
	Total	1686	1602	1504	1558
Location 9	Hourly	303[4]	307	320	398
	Salaried	32	35	38	53
	Total	335	342	358	451
Corporate	Hourly	8	10	11	11
	Salaried	35	35	35	36
	Total	43	45	46	47
Location 3	Hourly	122	167	201	218
	Salaried	22	32	36	34
	Total	144	199	237	252
Total Company	Hourly	5672	6706	6187	6174
	Salaried	842	796	765	752
	Total	6514	7502	6952	6926

NOTES

1. The information in this table was provided by the insurance manager of employer.
2. Counts as of June 7, 1998.
3. Employer acquired this division 8/28/94 but did not provide STD/LTD coverage until 1/1/96.
4. Coverage effective 10/1/97 for salaried and hourly employees.

WORKERS' COMPENSATION, SHORT-TERM DISABILITY AND LONG-TERM DISABILITY MATRIX[1]

	Workers' Compensation (WC)	Short-Term Disability (STD)	Long-Term Disability (LTD)
Definition	WC is the statutory benefit afforded to full- and part-time workers who sustain a work-related illness or injury.	STD is the wage replacement benefit provided for eligible employees who are unable to work for a specific period of time because of a nonwork-related health care problem.	LTD is the wage replacement benefit provided for eligible employees who meet medical criteria documenting their inability to work because of a nonwork-related health care problem. In most cases, LTD benefits commence when eligible employees have reached the time limit on STD.
Benefits	Though standards vary by state, wage replacement is usually calculated at $66^2/_3\%$ of the employee's wage; some employers subsidize this amount to 100%. WC also covers medical costs.	Plan determines the percent of usual wage and the duration of coverage (limited time frame, usual range is 13 to 52 weeks). Benefits, which start after waiting period (usually around seven days), cease with return to work at full duty or end of plan time limit, whichever comes first.	Plan determines rate of compensation (typically 50 to $66^2/_3\%$ of usual wage)[2] and the duration. Benefits cease with death, evidence of ability to return to work or satisfaction of retirement age.

WORKERS' COMPENSATION, SHORT-TERM DISABILITY AND LONG-TERM DISABILITY MATRIX[1]

	Workers' Compensation (WC)	Short-Term Disability (STD)	Long-Term Disability (LTD)
Nature of Benefits	Workers' compensation is "no fault," meaning it holds neither party (employee or employer) responsible for the cause of an accident or injury.[3] Employers fund the program with no employee contribution; premiums are based on employers' experience ratings.	Not mandated in most states, STD is funded by the employer, often as an incentive for employee recruitment and retention.	LTD is a voluntary plan funded by the employer. Some supplemental plans are employee funded.
Claims Management	Areas of concern in the management of WC claims are • Reporting and recording • Assignment—medical only, medical/indemnity • Compensability determination: investigation and documentation • Medical management • RTW philosophy • Setting of reserves • Indemnity calculation • Subrogation • Settlement • Litigation	Areas of concern in the management of STD claims are • Compensability determination: investigation and documentation • Use of independent medical examiners (IMEs) • RTW philosophy and continued employment • Closure	Areas of concern in the management of LTD claims are • Compensability determination: investigation and documentation • Monitoring • Vocational rehabilitation • Subrogation • RTW philosophy • Closure

WORKERS' COMPENSATION, SHORT-TERM DISABILITY AND LONG-TERM DISABILITY MATRIX[1]

	Workers' Compensation (WC)	Short-Term Disability (STD)	Long-Term Disability (LTD)
Regulations[4]	With jurisdictional variation, WC regulations affect • Insurance coverage—state pools or private • Communication—FROI, employee notification, access to and/or release of information, privacy concerns • Claims administration procedures including arbitration and settlement • Provider selection, MMI • Vocational rehabilitation • Managed care • Continued employment (employer generally restricted from firing employee with open claim) • Fiduciary issues—duties, contracts and registration and licensing requirements	Short-term disability is regulated under • ERISA • ADEA, ADA, Right to Privacy, HIPAA, FMLA (discrimination, accommodation of permanent disability, preexisting conditions exclusions) • State insurance laws	Long-term disability is regulated under • ERISA • Social Security, ADA

NOTES

1. Sharon E. Muran contributed most of the ideas incorporated in this matrix. A registered nurse with a master's degree in public health, Ms. Muran is an executive IDM consultant for Marsh Risk Consulting. She has specialized in case management, health care consulting, and disability prevention and management services based on managed care principles.

2. Recent changes are affecting LTD benefits. There is a growing trend to give employees the option of "having LTD premiums (employer paid) included in their paychecks as taxable income. Employee-paid plans are increasing in popularity. The advantage of these concepts is tax-free disability benefits. . . . The higher the income replacement, the more inviting for employees to go out on claim. Employees have a disincentive to return to work, and they are likely to stay out longer. In reality, the claimant's standard of living can actually be improved while on disability, if one considers the reduction in employment-related costs such as commuting, income taxes and Social Security or other payroll taxes." *The DMEC Times,* September 1998, 3, 6.

3. This does not mean the cause of an occupational injury or illness is unimportant. To prevent future accidents or illnesses (as well as to ensure OSHA compliance), an employer investigates and addresses the precipitating cause of a workers' compensation claim.

4. See "Chapter 4: Legal Issues" for a discussion of how state and federal laws regulate workers' compensation, short-term disability and long-term disability.

Glossary

Absence Management: Process of monitoring and controlling the use of unscheduled paid time off and of the Family and Medical Leave Act. Early identification of the reasons for absence from work enables appropriate and immediate intervention, which in turn reduces the risks for disability. Disability prevention is the primary goal of absence management.

Adjudication: Studying and settling a case; making a decision about a process.

Americans with Disabilities Act of 1990 (ADA): Federal law that protects qualified employees and job applicants who have disabilities. Rather than deny such people employment opportunities, an employer is required to make "reasonable accommodations" to their mental or physical impairments to enable them to perform essential job functions.

Appeals Process: ERISA procedure in which individuals covered by an employer-sponsored benefits plan can appeal a determination of benefits. Time limits apply to appeals, which must be filed within 60 days of determination.

Call Center: Phone center for common intake of claims information or, increasingly, absence information. By providing–through one toll-free number–a means to report all absences, employers attempt to address early the problems behind absence.

Case Management: Strategic approach that identifies, coordinates and evaluates the delivery of health care to an individual. The goal of case management is to improve care delivery, streamline and make more effective claims management and administration, and effectively return employees to work.

Casual Absence: An unscheduled absence classified as a personal day, sick day or paid time off.

Claim: Demand by an individual to recover compensation and/or medical expenses under a workers' compensation or nonoccupational disability policy. (The individual who submits a claim is known as a claimant.)

Claims Adjuster: Third party, usually independent, responsible for all aspects of claims management.

Claims Department: That part of an insurance company, third-party administrator or self-administered employer that pays and handles claims.

Claims Management: Comprehensive approach to processing claims that includes determination of compensability; initial and continuing assessment of an employee's disability; the coordination of payment (depending on benefit) for health care provider, rehabilitation treatment, time off and settlement for closure; and the determination of an employee's qualification for other benefit plan offsets.

Claims Reserve: The amount estimated to be necessary to cover future cost of claims.

Class: Group into which different types of work are classified for premium-rating purposes. Examples of classes are clerical/office, sales, warehouse, construction and manufacturing.

Communication: Exchange of information through writing, speech, signal or behavior. Effective communication requires not only good writing, speaking and, in the case of videos, acting skills, but also thoughtful reading and listening habits. In an integrated program, communication requires—between all parties—interactive loops of dispersed information and feedback.

Compensation Award: Order to pay compensation for a number of periods, either definite or indefinite, as the character of the injury requires. Compensation award can be paid in installments or as a lump sum.

Consolidated Omnibus Budget Reconciliation Act of 1985 (COBRA): Federal law that requires employers to offer continued health insurance coverage to eligible employees and their beneficiaries when their group health insurance coverage is terminated.

Consortium: The companionship of a spouse. A spouse may collect damages for the value of the other spouse's companionship, lost due to an accident or mental condition such as stress resulting from that accident.

Controverted Claim: Claim that has been denied.

Cost Containment (Medical): Methods and programs designed to contain costs by ensuring appropriateness, medical necessity and relatedness of treatment and procedures. Examples include utilization review and bill review.

Cost Drivers: The conditions and circumstances that, directly or indirectly, impact adversely on costs. Major cost drivers in managing disability are claims administration, medical (physiological) factors, the aging workforce, workplace culture, psychosocial circumstances and the environment.

Counsel: Legal advice; also, a lawyer or lawyers.

Current Procedural Terminology (CPT) Codes: List of descriptive terms and identifying codes for reporting medical services and procedures provided by health care providers. The terminology provides a uniform language that accurately designates medical, surgical and diagnostic services, thus providing an effective means for reliable nationwide communication among health care providers, patients and third parties.

Diagnosis Related Groups (DRGs): Classification system that groups patients' medical conditions into exclusive and exhaustive disease categories or groups. The system was developed at Yale University in the late 1970s. Medicare adopted it in 1983 as the basis for the prospective payment system for reimbursing hospitals. The DRG generally is assigned based on the primary and secondary diagnoses and patient age, so that cases within a group have a similar level of severity of illness and should have similar lengths of stay and resource requirements.

Disability: Functional limitation that impedes an employee's performance of the material duties of his or her normal job.

Disability Duration Guidelines: Guidelines on expected duration of disabilities according to diagnoses, symptoms, severity and occupational factors. They are used to determine expected return-to-work dates. Example: *The Medical Disability Advisor* by Presley Reed.

Disability Management: Process similar to case management but appropriately qualified to target individuals with specific diagnoses that require proactive, continued involvement to achieve optimum impact (i.e., timely return to work or medically necessary health care services provided in the safest, least restrictive setting).

Disability, Nonoccupational: See *Short-Term Disability* and *Long-Term Disability.*

Disability, Occupational: See *Workers' Compensation.*

Disability Pension: Pension annuity payable to an eligible employee who becomes disabled before normal retirement age.

Disability, Permanent-Partial (PPD): Condition that actually or presumptively results in permanent, partial loss of earning power. (See *Schedule Injury.*)

Disability, Permanent-Total (PTD): Condition that actually or presumptively results in the equivalent of a complete and permanent loss of earning power. Workers' compensation laws of many states specify that certain injuries (e.g., loss of sight, loss of both hands or legs) are considered permanent and total disabilities regardless of the injured person's ability to do some work. Compensation may be limited by maximum time or a maximum amount; if compensation is unlimited, it may run for life.

Disability, Temporary-Partial (TPD): Condition that results in a partial loss of earning power but from which recovery can be expected. Compensation generally is based on a percentage of the difference between the person's pre-injury wage and what can be earned in a disabled condition.

Disability, Temporary-Total (TTD): Condition that results in total disability but from which complete recovery and return to employment is expected. Benefits are payable under workers' compensation laws during disability, until the employee recovers and returns to employment.

Early Intervention: Start of case management (including stay-at-work or return-to-work efforts) as soon as possible after an injury or illness occurs. This type of intervention involves effective communication between all stakeholders in the case.

Earnings: Money derived from personal services; that is, salary, wages and commissions.

Employee Assistance Program (EAP): Employer-sponsored services designed to help employees and their families find solutions to personal or workplace problems. The program may assist with legal or financial issues, child-care or elder-care problems, substance abuse and psychological problems. EAPs may also address such areas as violence in the workplace and employee harassment.

Employee Retirement Income Security Act of 1974 (ERISA): Federal law that sets minimum standards for funding, vesting and terminating employer-sponsored pension plans. It mandates reporting and disclosure requirements for group life and health plans and addresses claims procedures, nondiscrimination rules and fiduciary responsibilities.

Employers' Liability Insurance: Insurance that provides protection for damages arising out of injuries to employees during the course of their work in cases not covered by workers' compensation laws.

Ergonomics: Discipline of restructure of the work environment, tools and equipment, and redesign of jobs to better accommodate an employee's capabilities.

Experience: The loss record of an insured. Can be expressed on a calendar-year or a policy-year basis.

Family and Medical Leave Act of 1993 (FMLA): Federal law that covers employers with more than 50 employees within 75 miles of the applicable worksite. FMLA requires employers to provide eligible employees with up to 12 weeks of unpaid leave in any 12-month period due to birth of a child, placement of a child for adoption or foster care, or "serious health conditions" of the employee, spouse, child or parent.

Fiduciary and Co-Fiduciary Responsibility: Employer's principal internal decision makers who have the ultimate discretionary authority in plan administration. Fiduciary functions are also often delegated to third-party administrators and other external providers. Some of the external administrative functions that may create fiduciary status in an integrated disability case include precertifications for medical procedures, level-of-care decisions, and claims processing and review. Also affecting integrated disability programs are state laws that adopt fiduciary standards of conduct for parties with a legal responsibility for administering assets and liabilities on behalf of another party.

First Report of Injury (FROI): The first report of an industrial accident that must be filed with the insurance carrier and, in most cases, the state workers' compensation board.

Functional Capacities Evaluation: Evaluation conducted by an occupational or physical therapist that determines an individual's ability to perform a full range of activities primarily as they relate to the individual's job. For example, how much can a person lift, stand, bend, climb or do fine hand motions?

Health Insurance Portability and Accountability Act of 1996 (HIPAA): Federal law mandating new benefit portability rules. HIPAA prohibits employer health plans from discriminating in eligibility, enrollment or cost based on health status; it also restricts the use of preexisting condition exclusions.

Health Maintenance Organizations (HMOs): Organizations that provide, offer or arrange for covered health services. For a fixed, prepaid premium, plan members receive a set of basic and supplemental health maintenance and treatment services.

Health-Related Productivity: Portion of an organization's total output that is directly affected by individual and organizational health.

Health Services Provider (Provider): Any person, firm, corporation, partnership, association, agency, institution or other legal entity providing a service related to the medical treatment of an injured or ill employee. This includes, but is not limited to, physicians, dentists, chiropractors, vocational rehabilitation counselors, osteopaths, pharmacists, physicians, podiatrists, physical therapists, occupational therapists, massage therapists, psychologists, durable medical equipment dealers, psychiatric social workers, optometrists, registered nurses, licensed practical nurses, spiritual healers, acupuncturists, Christian Science practitioners, and institutions such as hospitals, rehabilitation centers and outpatient surgery centers.

High Technologic Diagnostic Testing: High-cost diagnostic tests such as CAT scans, MRIs, arthoscopies and PETs. There are specific indications for these procedures, and approving their utilization *before* they are given is an effective means of cost containment.

Horizontal Integration: Coordination of some or all historically separate claims management systems or benefits such as sick time, salary continuation, STD, LTD, WC and group health.

Hospital Bill Audit: Identifying invalid or inaccurate hospital charges by either review of the hospital bill or on-site chart review at the hospital.

ICD-9 Codes: World Health Organization's 9th Revision of the *International Classification of Diseases.* ICD-9 codes classify morbidity and mortality information for statistical purposes, and for the indexing of hospital records by diseases and operations, for data storage and retrieval.

Incentive: Motivating factor for individuals or groups. While an incentive can be a punishment, such as the loss of a contract, it usually is an award. For example, the employer could use a monetary incentive (such as paying the provider's nondiscounted health care rate) for an employee's sustained return to work following a disability.

Incident, Occupational: Unforeseen, unintended event arising out of one's employment and resulting in injury or illness.

Incur: To become liable for a loss or expense.

Indemnity: In workers' compensation, the benefit paid to replace wages that have been lost due to an occupational injury or illness, up to a dollar maximum.

Independent Medical Evaluation (IME): Medical examination carried out by a board-certified, physician specialist (other than the employee's treating physician) for the purpose of resolving issues relating to a claim.

Industrial Accident: See *Occupational Accident.*

Integrated Disability Management (IDM): Single management system for occupational (workers' compensation) and nonoccupational (short-term and long-term) disability. Aspects of an IDM program include a single claims intake and notification process, a single claims management system, a common medical case management process, a common return-to-work program and a single database.

Job Analysis: Identification of the essential functions of an occupation to determine the skills required for successful job performance. Depending on its purpose, a job analysis may include information about the physical demands of the job, stress factors, work environment and physical hazards.

Job Conditioning: Regimen of progressive physical and/or psychological training that is oriented toward assisting a disabled employee to return to work.

Judgment: Adjudication for the payment of money.

Large Case Management: Case management for catastrophic injuries (e.g., extensive burns, multiple trauma). In these situations, case management should be initiated immediately after notification of the injury.

Liability: The condition of being bound by law and justice to do something that may be enforced in the courts. An obligation, usually financial. The probable cost of meeting an obligation.

Liability Insurance, Employers': See *Employers' Liability Insurance.*

Limited Employee Initial Provider Change: Restrictions on the frequency of, limits on the timing of, or conditions on employee change of treating provider. For example, the workers' compensation statute could require prior approval of the employer, the insurer or the workers' compensation agency to authorize a change.

Long-Term Disability (LTD): Benefit that replaces a percentage of income lost because a nonoccupational injury or illness prevents an employee from doing his job for an extended length of time. After a waiting period (often covered by a short-term disability plan), the employee is paid until he is no longer disabled, or until he retires or reaches a specific cutoff age or duration limit set by an employer's benefit plan.

Loss: A valid claim for recovery. Payments made in connection with a loss.

Loss Prevention: Actions taken to prevent injuries or illnesses from occurring. Wellness and safety programs are considered loss prevention actions.

Loss Run: Monthly report giving number of claims, type of injury, body part, medical costs and wage replacement cost reserve.

Malingering: Feigning disability.

Managed Care: Approach to health care cost containment that enables the payer to influence the delivery and quality of health services prospectively (that is, before the services are provided). The techniques used by managed care programs include case management, physician gatekeepers, provider networks and components of utilization review such as admission review, admission precertification, continued stay review, discharge planning and mandatory second-opinion programs.

Medicaid: Federal program (administered and partially paid for by participating state governments) that provides medical benefits to eligible low-income persons.

Medical Fee Schedule: List of the maximum recommended reimbursement for medical services. A fee schedule usually has two parts: a relative value scale and a monetary conversion factor. Still, some fee schedules list actual dollar amounts. Many workers' compensation fee schedules also establish guidelines for the payment of services. The guidelines may include limitations on the number of units of service, restrictions on the frequency of service, requirements for treatment plans and requirements for referrals.

Medical Management: Management that ensures individuals receive prompt, medically necessary care appropriate to the injury.

Medical Only: An industrial accident that results in medical costs only.

Medicare: Nationwide, federally administered health insurance that covers hospitalization, medical care and some related services for eligible individuals. Medicare is available to persons with disabilities after they have received disability benefits for 24 months.

Nondisabling Injury: An injury that does not cause loss of time.

Nonoccupational Disability: See *Short-Term Disability* and *Long-Term Disability.*

Nuisance Value: Not the true value of a claim but the amount that the insurer will pay because the claim is an annoyance or would cost more to adjudicate.

Occupation: Any meaningful work for which an employee is reasonably qualified in terms of training, education and experience.

Occupational Accident: Accident occurring in the course of employment and caused by inherent or related hazards.

Occupational Classification: Classification of occupations according to the degree of risk inherently involved in the practice of that occupation.

Occupational Disability: See *Workers' Compensation.*

Occupational Disease: Impairment of health caused by continued exposure to conditions inherent in a person's occupation.

Occupational Health: Identifiable status of physical, mental and emotional well-being of a specified group of employees.

Occupational Health Program: Employer initiative to protect the physical, mental and emotional well-being of a specified group of employees.

Occupational Therapist: Accredited individual skilled in the administration of treatment(s), prescribed by a physician or other health care provider, to individuals having a disabling disease or injury. Treatment is based on the utilization of activities that encourage physically and mentally impaired individuals to contribute to their recovery process. The focus is on the functional activities of daily living (ADL), such as communication, personal care and work.

Operations: Activities of the employer and employees in the conduct of a business.

Partnership: Cooperation of a related group of parties, such as employees, employers, insurers, risk managers and health care providers.

Permanent Partial Disability: See *Disability, Permanent-Partial (PPD).*

Permanent Total Disability: See *Disability, Permanent-Total (PTD).*

Physical Capacity: Capability of an employee to perform work activities and job tasks.

Physical Demand Components: Standardized system used by the U.S. federal government to describe the physical activities required by various occupations.

Physical Therapist: Accredited individual skilled in the application of physical agents, other than drugs, to facilitate recovery. These agents may include heat, electricity, light, water and physical massage manipulation. A major focus of physical therapy, under prescription from a physician, is the development of a program both formal and self-administered to achieve maximum physical restoration and function.

Physician: Any person licensed in medicine, surgery, osteopathy or osteopathic surgery.

Practice Protocols: Widely accepted medical treatment standards for specific diagnoses.

Preexisting Condition: A medical condition that existed prior to employment and/or prior to a new accident; this usually means the injury is not, or not solely, the result of the new accident.

Preferred Provider Organization (PPO): Network of medical care providers and facilities that agrees to discount its charges in return for a high volume of patients and prompt payment. Employers agree to channel their employees to the PPO network to receive a lower insurance premium. Employees can use providers outside the PPO but are encouraged by lower out-of-pocket costs (deductible and co-insurance percentages) to use PPO providers. In workers' compensation, employees do not share in out-of-pocket costs.

Prevention: Use of wellness programs to promote good health and of safety programs to reduce accidental and occupational disabilities.

Provider: See *Health Care Provider.*

Qualified Worker: Person (as defined by ADA) who can perform the reasonable functions of a job with or without essential accommodations. The qualified worker must meet the employer's job requirements for education, work experience, job skills and training.

Rating, Experience: See *Experience Rating.*

Rating, Retrospective: See *Retrospective Rating.*

Reasonable Accommodation: As defined by ADA, changes, modification or adjustments to the work environment that enable a qualified person with a disability to perform the essential functions of a job. Reasonable accommodations may be job restructuring, equipment modification or other work environment changes that do not alter the essential functions of a job.

Recovery: Portion of a loss that an insurance company obtains through subrogation from a third party. For example, if someone is injured on the job because a tool was defective, the manufacturer of the tool may be found liable for the injury and would then have to make restitution for workers' compensation payments.

Rehabilitation: Restoring or improving a person's functional capabilities, health or ability to perform useful and constructive activities.

Rehabilitation Management: A process of rebuilding. It is a blend of disability management that includes some of the elements of work hardening (or a similar service). The goal is to return the individual to the same job position whenever possible. Rehabilitation management encompasses a disability management perspective and goals, and requires case management attention.

Reserve: A booking liability that is set aside to meet future obligations.

Residual Market: See *Assigned Risk.*

Retrospective Rating: Technique that permits adjustments of the final premium due for the policy term, based on the loss experience of the insured during the period of protection, subject to maximum and minimum limits. The valuation of the losses and retrospective adjustments is generally done annually, over a three-to-five-year period following the end of the relevant policy year, until a final adjustment policy is made.

Return-to-Work Program: Modified work that is offered to an injured employee who has not achieved full recovery and is temporarily partially disabled. Modified duty may be any reasonable accommodation, including limited hours, modified tasks or alternative work. Key aspects include the temporary nature of the assignment and a gradual upgrading of work tolerance.

Salary Continuation: Employer plan that provides a payment to salaried employees during periods of injury and/or illness. The benefit amount may be controlled by length of service, job performance and/or union contracts. This discretionary benefit can be coordinated with workers' compensation and other disability benefits so as not to exceed the base salary of the employee.

Schedule Injury: An injury listed in a workers' compensation law for which specified compensation is payable regardless of whether or not the employee suffers a loss of earning power. For example, the loss of a finger or toe.

Second-Injury Fund: A state fund designed to protect employers from being penalized for hiring a previously-injured worker, and to protect employees from discrimination. All employers contribute to this fund.

Short-Term Disability (STD): Benefit that replaces a percentage of income lost because a nonoccupational injury or illness prevents an employee from doing his job. After a short waiting period (e.g., a week), the employee is paid until he is no longer disabled, until he reaches the maximum coverage period or until he becomes eligible for LTD benefits.

Sick Pay: Employer-paid benefit for periods of illness. The benefit period is usually short, and eligibility is coordinated with other benefits (such as short- and long-term disability) to provide a range of coverage to the employee.

Social Security Offset: Offset allowed to workers' compensation benefits when an injured employee is also receiving Social Security or retirement disability benefits.

Stair Stepping or Stepladder Reserves: Unacceptable practice of routinely increasing the reserve without proper evaluation.

Subrogation: The right of an insurance company to receive from a third party the amount paid under a policy. See *Recovery*.

Third-Party Action: An action brought by the insurer or self-insured against a party, other than the insured or the employee, for recovery of workers' compensation monies.

Third-Party Administrator: See *Claims Adjuster*.

Total Cost of Disability: The sum of direct and indirect costs (also referred to as hidden costs), which includes medical payments; lost-time, overtime and replacement wages; administrative and disability management costs; insurance payments; litigation expense; training costs; and the costs associated with lost productivity, lower employee morale and reduced customer satisfaction.

Total Disability: See *Disability, Permanent-Total (PTD)* and *Disability, Temporary-Total (TTD)*.

Total Health Management: The coordination of horizontally integrated programs (incorporating nonoccupational disability, occupational disability and group health) with a vertically integrated system (primary through tertiary prevention).

Transitional Work Program: Training and development program to facilitate employees to return to modified work. Transitional work typically bridges an employee's capabilities during disability with those in full recovery. Transitional work is generally less physically or mentally demanding than an employee's previous job, and is modified by restructuring jobs or work stations, employing assistance devices, changing work hours, reducing work hours or assigning employee to a different job.

Treating Provider: Health care practitioner who has primary responsibility for the health care of an injured worker. For the purposes of this book, health care providers are eligible to be treating providers if a workers' compensation jurisdiction authorizes them to deliver health care services and products to an injured worker without an order, a referral or the supervision of another provider. Nonphysicians such as dentists, optometrists, chiropractors and psychologists can qualify as treating providers.

Usual and Customary (U&C); Usual, Customary and Reasonable (UCR); or Usual, Customary, Reasonable and Prevailing (UCRP): System that limits reimbursements to some uniform standard of prevailing provider charges. Each health care provider has a usual, a customary and an actual charge for each procedure. Reimbursement is limited to the lowest of these three charges. Usual and customary charges are common in health benefits; they are becoming more so in workers' compensation.

Utilization Review (UR): Formal assessment of the necessity and appropriateness of health care services; it is performed on a prospective (before health care is delivered), concurrent (during the provision of the health care) or retrospective (after the care has been delivered) basis. The assessment/review process is typically conducted telephonically by a nurse who gathers information from employee/provider/carrier about the health care service or procedure and the clinical setting. It is then determined whether established guidelines and clinical criteria support the health care services proposed or delivered.

- **Inpatient or In-Hospital UR:** Inpatient or in-hospital UR is conducted to assess medical necessity of care and appropriateness of the treatment setting. It is typically done for those conditions that require a hospital stay in excess of 24 hours. For example, this review would be done for an individual who may require hospitalization for a back problem such as a herniated vertebral disk with neurologic complications.

- **Outpatient and/or Ambulatory UR:** Outpatient UR is primarily conducted to assess the necessity and appropriateness of health care for conditions (such as an arthoscopic knee procedure or carpal tunnel release) that do not require a hospital stay that exceeds 23 hours. Outpatient UR is often referred to as *Ambulatory UR* and includes the review of those services often delivered in a health care provider's office or a clinic setting. Services such as physical therapy, occupational therapy, chiropractic care as well as high-tech, high-cost diagnostic procedures including MRI, CAT scan and myelogram are reviewed prospectively or retrospectively.

Vertical Integration: Coordination of all programs related to illness and injury, from prevention to return to work. With improved communication among the various groups (such as the medical department, line supervisor, employee, claims administrator and health care provider), vertical integration results in opportunities for injury prevention, disability reduction and cost control.

Vocational Rehabilitation: Process initiated as early as possible for any individual who requires evaluation and retraining for a job outside his current employ. The goal is to return the individual to appropriate, gainful, alternate work in as timely a manner as possible.

Wellness Program: Employer-sponsored program that intends to increase employees' quality of life, prevent illness and injury, maintain health, and reduce costs associated with illness and injury.

Work Hardening: The structuring of activities in order to maintain and improve the physical and psychological capabilities of a disabled employee. During work hardening (a concept related to job accommodation), injured employees return to their regular jobs on a reduced schedule (in keeping with their medical restrictions). The number of scheduled hours gradually increases as the employee's medical condition improves.

Workers' Compensation: State-mandated system in which employers are responsible for the cost of health care and wage replacement for employees with occupational illnesses or injuries. Employers pay regardless of who is at fault for the accident or illness, while employees, in general, may not sue even if employers have been negligent.

Workplace Culture: Company's values and priorities, which are demonstrated, in part, through its safety, health and disability management (including return-to-work) programs.

Index

L

S

Service providers
  partner selection, 90-91
  provider selection score sheet, 115-128
  provider reference questions, 129
Services agreement, 51-52

T

Total health management, 14-15
Training *see* IDM training table

W

Workers' compensation, 53-54
  communication responsibility for injuries, 138-139
  WC, short-term disability and long-term disability matrix, 196-199